Rethinking Subalternity
in Central and Eastern Europe

Rethinking Subalternity in Central and Eastern Europe

Francesco Trupia

TRANSNATIONAL PRESS LONDON
2020

PLACE AND SPACE SERIES: 02

Rethinking Subalternity in Central and Eastern Europe
By Francesco Trupia

Copyright © 2020 Transnational Press London

All rights reserved. This book or any portion thereof may not be reproduced or used in any manner whatsoever without the express written permission of the publisher except for the use of brief quotations in a book review or scholarly journal.

First Published in 2020 by TRANSNATIONAL PRESS LONDON in the United Kingdom, 12 Ridgeway Gardens, London, N6 5XR, UK.
www.tplondon.com

Transnational Press London® and the logo and its affiliated brands are registered trademarks.

Requests for permission to reproduce material from this work should be sent to: sales@tplondon.com

Paperback
ISBN: 978-1-912997-45-9

Cover Design: Gizem Çakır
Cover Photo: Violeta Apostolova: The spinning wheel, the Open Air Ethnographic Museum "Etar", Bulgaria.

www.tplondon.com

CONTENT

About the Author ii
PREFACE 3
INTRODUCTION. Philosophy and Minority Studies. What is at Stake? 7
Part I: GENESIS, MATERIALISATION, BOUNDARIES, AND MEANINGS OF "MINORITY" AS SUBALTERN OTHERNESS
CHAPTER ONE. Setting the Scene 19
CHAPTER TWO. Minority Identities in Central and Eastern Europe: A Critical Overview 25
CHAPTER THREE. Post-Communism and Post-Colonialism: Do They Mirror Each Other? 51
Part II: THE MAKING AND THE RE-MAKING OF SUBALTERNS: A GRAMSCIAN PERSPECTIVE
CHAPTER FOUR. Antonio Gramsci and Subaltern Cultures: Fundamental Remarks 73
CHAPTER FIVE. 1989 "Organic Crisis" and Post-Communist Positionality of Minority Groups 81
CHAPTER SIX. "(Re-)thinking Subalternity and the Necessity of Hegemony 103
CHAPTER SEVEN. Gramsci's Way Out: Subaltern Mobilisation and the Role of Intellectuals 117
CHAPTER EIGHT. The Paradox of Hegemonic (In-)Tolerance 131
CHAPTER NINE. Gramscianism: Marxism Otherwise? 143
OPEN CONCLUSIONS
CHAPTER TEN. In Search of a New Praxis 151

ABOUT THE AUTHOR

Francesco TRUPIA holds a PhD in Philosophy from Sofia University "St. Kliment Ohridski", Bulgaria. Since 2014, he has mainly worked as a researcher in Armenia, Bulgaria and Kosovo for international think-tanks and as a NGO practitioner. His research interests lie in Political Philosophy and Theory of Politics with regard to contested identities of minority groups and radical democracy in post-Communist countries.

PREFACE

This study aims to philosophically investigate the notion of 'subalternity' with regard to a variety of minority issues in Central and Eastern Europe. Although a lot has been written about, too little has been achieved in practice. Therefore, this monograph gives a different perspective over the notion of "minority" in the attempt to reopen new and old places of confrontation that would potentially diversify scholarly trajectories of critical investigation.

For the purpose of this study, Antonio Gramsci's subtle, and philosophically sophisticated, Theory of Hegemony has helped me to bring to the foreground the most debated issues at stake. Through the lens of Gramsci's philosophy of praxis, which has been barely applied and practically developed with success, the slippery terminology of Gramscianism is here employed to offer new opportunities to unpack sociological and cultural dilemmas in the attempt to shed light on conundrums of liberal democracy, overlooked facets of minority identities and behaviour patterns across the post-Communist region.

In the first part of this monograph, I touch upon scholarly concerns that have so far dealt theoretically with the issues of minority groups. To begin with, I particularly focus on the activity of naming multifaceted specificities of collective entities. This theory-oriented analysis goes on with the attempt to point out how "minority" has been negatively used as a term for labelling marginality and exclusion from the core society. Drawing attention to the paradigm of "cultural identity", the latter seems currently challenged by newly-arrived minorities after being correctly used in the aftermaths of the horrific experience of the Second World War. Mistakenly, in my opinion, this paradigm refers largely to the old-fashioned notion of "ethnos" and thereby ascribes upon the nature and issues of a minority group in question, and the multiple layers and intersectional aspects that the latter might be composed of.

Given this token, the first part is devoted to confronting the three most employed "academic silos" — namely, "essentialism", "constructivism", and "poststructuralism", also well-known as "postmodernism". Along their scholarly trajectories, the philosophical branch of post-colonial studies is used for investigating to what extent the post-Communist democracy transition reflects and contains post-colonial phenomena typically salient in the Global South. Aware of the fact that such approach would be extremely criticised in the specific context of post-Communist CEE, in my opinion a non-chronology-centred notion of the 'post' shows how a certain parallelism between post-coloniality and the post-Communism is nothing but an attempt to critically highlight how the arrival of Western-style liberal democracy in the region has provided a new venue for historically marginalised communities to be recognised and heard, to have their legitimate interests and identities respected, and to contest inherited practices, rules, and narratives excluding or disadvantaging them (Kymlicka and Bashir 2008: 2). Yet, practices of exclusion which discredit and repudiate have never ceased to be put at work, enduring and lingering effects against the full-fledged democracy transition and thereby impinging on creating a society of equal citizens. Without any doubt, this post-colonial paradigm has little to do with the notion of de-colonial. While the latter remains a political option against the status quo, the former is here employed for looking differently at it. From a "minority perspective" I wish to keep such post-colonial perspective as the relevant cipher for unravelling fabrication and experiences of exclusion and marginalisation that have been instrumentally, subtly and implicitly reorganised to set the "alien Other" apart. In other words, going along the large-scale trajectory of post-1989 events up until present-day affairs, the post-colonial view becomes the instrument for not only reading the genesis of the above-mentioned fabrication of exclusion and marginalisation of certain segments of society, but also for understanding its trajectory in time and space.

Hence, the second part of this monograph moves forward to unpack specific-group dynamics with regard to minority identities and historical contingencies. The post-colonial paradigm reviews the societal role of minority groups, of their identities, of their behaviour patterns. Drawing on Antonio Gramsci's (slippery) terminology, this second part focuses on the term "subaltern" rather than "minority". In the attempt to unravel more and more the human condition of marginalisation and exclusion of certain segments of society, whose marginality stems from hegemonic cultural domination, the use of the term "subalternity" (Spivak 1999, among others) is employed for opening up new philosophical perspectives in CEE. In doing so, while the term "subaltern" becomes the vector by which unpacking the legacy of post-Communist coloniality, "subalternity" facilitates the understanding of minority positionality throughout society. Within the framework of post-colonial studies, the term "subaltern" sheds light on historical contingencies of minority groups after the backdrop of the Communist regime across the region. In this, Gramsci's formulation of "organic crisis" allows an interpretation of the post-1989 events in the form of ideological continuum of power and hegemonity brought anew to work thanks to the reversal of the relationship of forces organised around usurpation of power and an appropriation of a vocabulary turned against those who had once possessed it and used it. In other words, a feeble emerging domination that poisoned itself as it grew lax, entering into domination in a new space of existence by masking itself as another (Focault 1997:157) despite continuing to last subtly under the stucco façade of democracy. Hence, Gramsci's Theory of Hegemony helps to confront minority issues in tandem with the constantly colonialising manoeuvres of identity-forming that have definitely penetrated the realm of everyday life of subalterns, who, paradoxically, have in turn accepted them in order to get benefits out of them. This arguably implausible, albeit fascinating, interpretation of post-1989 events in CEE does not exclusively aim at paving the way toward a revolutionary journey of those who fell under the trap of subalternity. In fact, following once again Gramsci, this monograph aims to define hegemony as a "perspective of opportunities" for subalterns. Hegemony, if understood dialectically, shows from within its power structures, from which political and cultural hegemony begins vertically to fuction throughout society even prior than its manifestations appear on the territorial (e.g., centralisation), political (e.g., vertical structures of power) or legal ground (e.g., violation of human rights). This proposed theoretical tandem between the post-1989 "organic crisis" and hegemony leads toward yet another fundamental aspect of the Gramscian legacy: the "formation of intellectuals" and their role in society. For the purpose of this study, a distinction among those that Gramsci referred to as "organic intellectuals" and "traditional ones" is made, looking through a wide range of intra-minority group dynamics. Avoiding any economics-related specificity, the dichotomy of "organic" and "traditional" intellectualism focuses on the societal role that the first group (e.g., politicians, representatives, NGO practitioners, and cultural leaders) may (not) entertain with the second one (e.g., ordinary people, "minorities-within a-minority", etc.).

In conclusion, the final part of this study questions the contemporary credibility of the philosophical foundations that liberal multiculturalism is based on. In particular, the philosophical enquiry is directed to understand whether or not liberal multiculturalism can be still considered a valid answer to minority issues and sustainable model for the accommodation of not-yet-pacified concerns and newly arrived claims. In light of the increasing critical positions against liberal multiculturalism as a whole, the main accusation of this monograph is directed toward the subtle form behind which liberal multiculturalists have veiled themselves by imposing a hegemonic discourse pre-empted of any sort of confrontation between different societal groups (König 2002). By having contributed to fertilising the terrain for the rise of "ethnicism" and its contemporary quasi-fascist narratives, this monograph scholarly accuses liberal multiculturalism of having reintroduced a new kind of differentiation among groups (e.g., "meta-racism"; see Salecl 1994: 11--9) and disguised real social problems through a form of new communitarianism in which the power of the community's leaders has been imposed through practices and prohibitions on behalf of those members whose claims of recognition have been substituted by the approval of particularities opposed to the idea of parity (Touraine 2007: 145-147). In this, the possible pitfall to employ "cultural identity" as a paradigm might tend easily to fail with regard to subaltern (minority) groups. Recalling the first part of the monograph, such paradigm shows all its weaknesses. By pre-empting de facto all potential conditions of equal parity and recognition in the public realm by not treating all cultures as equally valuable, it essentialises features of "culture" and "identity" in search of proper recognition and accommodation which are possible insofar as differences project themselves in the form of "otherness". In the very end, this final accusation goes thus against the model of liberal multiculturalism, whose asymmetries of (externally imposed) recognition do not set up an enrichment between peoples and cultures with an equal right to life. On the contrary, they introduce the superiority of the "tolerator" toward "others" to be tolerated and accepted as long as they remain in the position of "the Other". Again this, Gramsci's "circle of humanity", is a new (decolonised) space of recognisability of all people whom we have not heard of before, and who deserve to be heard of, along with their history, their literature, and their culture.

INTRODUCTION

Philosophy and Minority Studies. What is at Stake?

The global financial crisis that since 2007 began to destabilise the economic security of the richest and the fastest developing countries of the world, also started to undermine fundamental principles that liberal democracies were organised around. Today's phenomena of populism, which definitely show the deep crisis of the liberal model of democracy worldwide, are interfering along with the transition of Central and Eastern Europe toward a wealthier region of full-fledged democracies. Three decades onwards the opening of the gateway to Europe, that collective sense of hope and euphoria that arose after the fall of the first brick of the Berlin Wall, seems to have been lost along the way. The large variety of cultural demands and related political campaigns for a better democracy have inflamed the everyday discourse in the wider public of all post-Communist democracies. Mainly on the asset of identity, the loudest voices of liberation and securitisation have paradoxically won the ground in support of ethnocentric, nationalist, nativist, and alt-right claims and policies rather than confronting the visibly corrupted power structures, the ossification of their hierarchies, and those practices of doing politics that have set apart and thereby marginalised specific segments of society.

All of these have partially proven untrue Francis Fukuyama's prevision on the prevailing strength of liberal values over the potential attempts to bring the world back to authoritarianism. In the post-Communist Europe, those flags of nationalism that hung unnoticed on the public buildings and were kept hidden behind the stucco façade of democracy transition, are nowadays waving with fervent passion (Billig 1995) after being culturally discredited and politically kept in check (Fukuyama 2018: 62). Aimed at protecting society from unsettled and not completely pacified issues within the countries, or from the return to a post-modern "Socialist melting pot", today's forms of populism do not show a defined political force and a coherent political style (Rancière 2016: 102). However, they own the quintessentially political property of dismissal of otherness, and a political discourse that continues to rhetorically ascribe ethnic, gender, nowhereness, and strict blood features, or lack of particular skills and inability to participate, upon "the

Other". If discursively populist fabrication of inferiority might be scholarly seen as yet another theme for discussion in the field of identity politics, the latter has so far shown nothing but a descriptive narration of issues that subaltern groups are affected by. Vernacularism and banal representation of Otherness have not stopped malignant associations of Roma groups with ideas of nowhereness, of refugees and migrants with laziness, of ecological struggles with frivolousness, and so forth. Swinging between the hot and the banal, the collective hysteria as well as anguish and economic uncertainty are currently mobilised to keep the stew of the "Other within" or "upcoming Other" boiling. It follows that serious practices for accommodation of diversities and recognition in the public sphere have been largely overlooked or poorly considered in defence of certain rules that liberal democracies should stand for (e.g., neutrality of the State, private/public dimension of claims, rule of law, and so forth). Nevertheless, imposition of certain stigmas throughout society and banal representation of taxonomy of peoplehood have never ceased to work within the realm of everydayness.

While in many parts of the world the long aftermath of the Second World War was (arguably) characterised by a consolidation of democratic States embedded in universal ideas of individual rights, in post-Communist Europe the problem of diversity has been as puzzling as challenging (Cornel and Hartmann 1998: 9). The dissolution of the Eastern bloc paved the way to the idea that privatisation and liberal market would succeed by default to soften the pre-existing economic differences, the scarcity of resources and the poor standards of living. Moreover, protection of marginalised groups and regulation of minority rights would become important indicators for tracking the structural transition toward a full democratisation. In this respect, Yugoslavia's successor States began to attempt to guarantee protection and recognition to minority groups in order to fulfil parameters of conditionality to secure their access to the European Union. Similarly, post-Soviet Republics and post-Communist States had immediately started to theorise model security management for confronting the brutal logic of violence erupted on the road to full-fledged democracy standards. In fact, territorial proximity of kin-States has historically been the major issue, whereby protection of the newly-achieved post-Communist statehood and principle of sovereignty began to be put at stake by breakaway minority entities.

As a matter of fact, rather than a fairly-driven discourse of, and for, confrontation over the subject-matter, the question of whether or not detoxicated patriots can stop getting high and offset the balkanisation of modern life and allow still-repressed cultures to rise to their selfdetermination (Matuštík 1993: 22) remains still the central enquiry. Some continue to pay attention to the normative facets of minority identities and claims in order to firstly soften concerns of integration, inclusion, and coexistence and only secondly contribute for the better to the arena of democratic, pluralistic society. Others stand in opposition to such cheap promotion of diversity, thereby looking beneath the surface of not-yet-recognised sub-national/cultural groups and their identities in order to leave room for further debates over public legitimisation. Both positions have remained quite confrontational either in support of multiculturalism or in opposition to such model of society. It followed that several questions have been critically raised in regard to legitimacy of cultural rights in the wider public, and how minority groups may validly construct their claims and demands in order to legitimately seek out full recognition within the larger society. In this, due to highly controversial vis-à-vis confrontation, they have utterly failed to call for a concrete implementation of multicultural policies (MCPs).

In between, however, yet another approach has found voice. Discrediting the above-mentioned dichotomy, particular attention has been critically oriented toward those "not-yet-recognised" or "newly-arrived" minority groups. Despite the fact that they have always existed, they have recently manifested how they could represent a double-edged sword for the wider public. Of particular interest is how any group identity could either potentially be a resource or a handicap, beneficial or inflammatory aspect for boosting diversity and testing the level of tolerance within a society and even into a homogeneous cluster of people. This angle of investigation digs deeper into the sphere of the so-called "cultural identity" with the attempt to investigate seriously the carrier of both terms and understand what might potentially impinge on our contemporary societies.

To a certain extent, it is possible to notice how philosophical investigation within and across newly-arrived (sub-)disciplines related to the topic of minority issues (e.g., Gender Studies, Media Studies, or Minority Studies) has definitely brought these sub-cultures and interdisciplinary approaches at the centre of the philosophical inquiry in the same way the post-1989 events in history and minority actors, local communities, and others alike have done so far. The first approach has generally dealt with an epistemological investigation of the ways communitarian claims are formulated and conveyed into the public sphere (Jürgen Habermas, Nancy Fraser, among others), or how each (hegemonic) power system organised around a majoritarian cultural system would eventually accommodate minority claims (Kymlicka

1992). At the same time, the second approach digs ontologically into what influences the realm of everyday life, whereby intersubjective relations and respective "identities" never cease to be influential and confrontational (e.g., radical democracy). Without any doubt, this field of research has been the one preferred by critical philosophy and its scholars while working on different branches of socio-cultural implications.

In regard to the issues of minority groups, traditional approaches used in social sciences remain very incomplete in their methods of investigation. Especially in Central and Eastern Europe in the post-1989 era, disciplines such as political science, anthropology, or sociology have largely come to accept a linear as well as teleological conception of modernity. They have embarked on a mission to shed light on how the post-Communist region would promote a cultural management model for overcoming civilisational deficiencies and finally reaching the stage of modernity and liberal democracy (Kušić, Lottholz, and Manolova 2019). However, as the French philosopher François Lyotard has noticed, traditional approaches are nowadays in danger of being incorporated into the programming of the social whole as a simple tool for the optimisation of its performance; this is because its desire for a unitary and totalising truth lends itself to the unitary and totalising protection of the system's managers (1983: 12). In other words, the story of all disciplines tells at once the story of their lamentably fragmented knowledge and of their steady convergence into a unity at the same time, as the insights of the more fundamental fields (Kramnick 2017: 69). Thus, some continue to criticise anthropology for constantly positing "minority groups" in terms of otherness and cultural alterity in their wider analyses. In political science, too, the term "minority" has been reduced to a simply instrumental illustration of how greatly schematised definitions society employs for certain groups or segments of society itself. In doing so, the analyses of discursive strategies in politics have drawn attention to how politicians' lexicon, media coverage and official documents refer to minority groups in terms of "subaltern" or "inferior" for evidently different purposes. In legal terms, too, recognition of the term in official declarations, conventions, and motions has been recently challenged by the rise of the intersectional and overlapping aspects of minority identities that have not yet found space in the national and international jurisprudence due to legal vacuum. Of particular interest is the growth of use of terms such as "caste", "class", "race", and "gender", whose reference to a "minority" has been so far used as an only quintessentially political concept, most effectively rhetorically in the political discourse. In anthropological terms, this large variety of "minority facets" seems to have called for the need of a "true anthropology". The latter would benefit from looking, listening, and even writing about sensitive events that happen in dusty streets of a neighbourhood, by a crowded bus stop in the morning, in a shabby room, at a roundtable organised at regular intervals, in a room-sized office, or on a social media platform for articulating and hearing opinions, needs, and interests of communities. In other words, a "true anthropology" would avoid filtering human everydayness through a panoptic position in order to better investigate despite the fact that the latter would mean to renounce the apodistic claims of the metaphysical school (Didi-Huberman 2016: 65–87). Similarly, sociology can dismantle the discursive construction of a given minority as "something alien" to pave the way to a different perspective from the one of the marginalised, excluded, or culturally leading-threat entity (Glavanakova 2016:46). Across both disciplines, ethnographers are often found involved in constantly exploring diverse issues for venturing the parapet of social constructs and understanding deeper the complexity of doing ethnographic research. According to the highly normative framework that post-Communist Eastern European countries began to deal with, minority issues would paradoxically result from the same overwhelming approach of law aimed at attempting to develop a sustainable and equal theory of recognition and accommodation in order to not impinge on civil liberties or infringe human rights. It follows that theorisation of multicultural forms of citizenship (Kymlicka 1994), among other things, has been more investigated through law-centred meaning, genesis, boundaries, and materialisation of citizenry. Within contested nations, especially those rumoured to be on the shores of structural change, a scholarly strategy to leave behind law-oriented framework might open up an interesting angle of investigation. Following Michael Foucault's work on biopolitical citizenship (mentioned by Gržinić 2019: 184), conceptualisation of minority groups and cultural claims can be easily detached from law-oriented theories in contemporary democracies. Yet, even in this case social sciences and humanities often show their own hidden lacunae, whose nature is due to accidents of their formation (Birnaum 2016) and typical features that ought to be discarded for getting at something that is more scholarly useful than accurate. In general, social sciences and sub-disciplines seem to increasingly reshape the explanatory frameworks of the fields they support (Kramnick 2017: 69). Above all, the major issue concerns the almost complete withdrawal of those figures who had welcomed the arrival of new forms of diversity by ethically motivating the public realm to new forms of resilience and respect towards everyone's culture. However, although social sciences continue correctly to address scholarly inevitable questions and desire and ethical motivation by which they are driven since the beginning of the 1990s, they seem to have lost their philosophical horizon(s). This lack of the practical use of the "queen of sciences", namely, of philosophy, as Theodor W. Adorno used to define it (mentioned by A. Birnbaum 2016: 16), has somewhat left almost vacant the space for the search of those answers that peculiar issues of contemporary, multicultural societies deserve currently to find answers for. Among a large number of issues, the never-ending debate over the issue of identity stands by in a waiting room open to the disposal of political opportunism as well as power-related discursive strategies. This does not only impinge on the real understanding of the current state of affairs, but it discredits what philosophy can contribute to. Apparently prepared for gently avoiding serious questions, supporters of liberal multiculturalism have started to refuse to deal with extremely debated condundrums and paradoxes stemming from their own theories. An avoidance that has become the sole business of philosophy (Murray 2018: 224), replaced by a descriptive methodology as the only possible strategy of investigation. The latter lacks of critical responsibility, which should be taken instead into consideration in politics as well as in academia and even beyond.

Therefore, a philosophical investigation can neither anticipate normative facets of a new theory to come nor reject in toto the idea to present one's cultural identity in a non-negotiable manner (Waldron 2000a). Philosophy is here aimed at what is not a priori given and not authorised or under control. Since philosophy successfully unravels the sphere of the tabooed and the controlled, the latter offers knowledge of reality. The latter is viewed as an object distanced from itself through a cognitive approach that brings reality to show itself (Tillich 2000: 23). Rather than the (new) social sciences, whose academic intervention has so far contributed to only describe the state of affairs, perhaps philosophical investigation can better disentangle, unravel and shed light on internalities and externalities that compose the reality of contemporary societies. In fact, the main aim of investigating philosophically social groups, such as minority groups, is that of going beyond what easily appears and is taken for granted in the wider public as a result of the political games or normal development and consequences of previous events. Especially in those societies that remain currently highly contested and deeply divided from within, where issues of social justice, recognition, and pre-emerging culture are at stake, philosophy is a precisely fresh-looking instrument for understanding in space and time a wealth of internally hidden and externally confused interconnectedness of societal links, cultural bonds, and political boundaries that reflect peoples within the context they posit themselves and interact. Once again, philosophy implies a different strategy, whose purpose is based on the revolutionary force of the reversal — that is, the political stake to transform the thoughtlessness and vernacularism of the realm and its academic disciplines of any matter, into a thinking-as-acting, which is nothing but a reflective intervention for affirming the politicality of the realm itself and thereby occupy actively what, otherwise, would merely remain inhabit or malignantly manipulated (Marchart 2018: 191; Althusser 1976: 38). As time has passed by, experts and commentators and scholars have found useless the post-1989 highly politicised and ethnically divisive nomenclature "majority" and "minority". In light of the wealth of transformations that civic communities, political organs, and minorities, in general, have gone through, philosophy is strategically useful to turn the investigation into the ontological ground, whereby it is possible to reject and precisely distinguish the "real" from the "constructed" forms of identities (Cheskin 2016: 28) – no matter if from the social majority or minority.

At the same time, such proposed philosophical investigation does not dismiss other disciplines from the academic horizon(s) and scholarly perspective(s), but it would challenge some older configuration of the disciplines that have so far mistakenly or inefficiently depicted the contemporary society. In the very end, a philosophical investigation does not even negatively perpetuate the conviction that overcoming boundaries between disciplines or ruling over the integration of different fields of studies is necessary since they no longer fit rigorous methodologies or too much scholarly nimbleness. Some would recognise the best way to be interdisciplinary as an academic habit to fully focus on one's discipline and model. In simpler words, a horizontal approach of investigation which lets disciplines interact with each other without any restriction of movement. In this regard, such "interdisciplinarity" is seen as a reductive multiplicity of methods, arguments, and norms to retain. On the contrary, others affirm that the world does not have a single order that is reducible to one discipline rather than another. It is true that an object of investigation, such as a specific minority group or related culture and identity, could be known from an interdisciplinary viewpoint at its own level of explanation. In this case, political science or anthropology are equally credited to explain, as they do equally, the real state of affairs. As Kramnick states, this ontological pluralism (2017: 68) creates a common groundwork of explanation by linking facts and fact-based theories across the disciplines they have been investigated in. Following this approach, however, the behaviour patterns of minority members explained by sociologists, for example, would refer to, and be limited by, the explanation of the same behaviour patterns studied by ethnologists or anthropologists. To a certain extent, it should be noted how this only explanation of an object of investigation results from the modus operandi of disciplines that reveal in turn the features they have because of the accidents of their formations mentioned above.

Nevertheless, all of these revitalise seriously philosophy and put it in the centre of discussion, on a methodological, academic and practical level. In its full capacity to relate to the "new" in its newness, as Adorno pointed out (Birnaum 2016: 16), philosophy relates the former with the latter without seeking to innovate academic investigation over the so-called "minority studies" into a new discipline in Europe and beyond. Despite the fact that a large number of scholars and academics have found shortcomings in new interdisciplinary approaches, in which — they strongly believe — the philosophical horizon is lost (Bogomilova 2016:19), philosophy stands for a method of critical investigation that goes beyond social sciences. In fact, philosophy transcends overall specificities as well as academic separations between them, avoiding irrelevancy of enquiries in the attempt to give a fresh look upon them. It enables investigation from below and in between internalities and externalities of the subject-matter, according to which a philosophical investigation is not only employed for being a leading-instrument of interaction between disciplines that deal with minority issues, but also it emphasises the necessity to transcend historically distorted and imposed logics of concept by disentangling narrowed categories of being, upon which specific knowledge has been ascribed and categorised. So far, for example, categories of diversity have followed ethnic and racial points of reference in sociological context, overlapping the fields of political science, anthropology, religious studies, and so forth. Philosophy cannot here be organised as, or identified with, a separation of disciplines that merely occludes a vocation restored by the project of interdisciplinary studies, branding the same "disciplines" tending to almost vanish, or last in contradiction, more quickly than they seem to handle the current investigation. Being at the core of discussion, philosophy neither unravels the real issues by interplaying the role of mediator between disciplines, nor posits itself as a new discipline. Philosophy must be here rescued from the ongoing academic decadence, in which disciplines aim only to create borders and surround themselves with "new studies" in order to receive grants, get research proposals approved, and have their projects accepted. Against this pitfall, the force of philosophy lies in its attitude to avoid institutionalisation as well as standardisation of methodological investigation in accepting an externally imposed, predefined, and ascribed matter assigned to a concept. It rather does without, for the sake of the obscure lure of the object (Birnbaum 2016: 24).

By default, the so-called field of "minority studies" cannot be excluded from being investigated by philosophy. The imperative need for a philosophical investigation of the complexity of the subject-matter brings the actuality of philosophy itself among all disciplines. In its attempt to achieve an "ethics of dialogue", philosophy allows, if and only if applied, a separation of branches of specialised studies limited within theology or constructed by political discourse strategies for example, in turn, connected with a specific religion or taxonomy of peoplehood. In this regard, philosophy practices the unknown—namely, the reverse identificatory logic of the object of investigation—thereby highlighting its non-identical aspects and thereby coordinating the paths towards a precise and conjectural answer to "when" (e.g., history), "where" (e.g., places of existence) and "who" (e.g., subjectivity), rather than only "what". Therefore, philosophical enquiry as an instrument of investigation goes across and beyond social sciences and tackles their limitations. It actually asks who takes identity for granted or gets benefit from it; who is passionate about it and who manipulates it; who mobilises by a sense of national identification and when; who rejects such a framework and, on the contrary, tries to best understand the bigger picture in order to address the complex question of "why".

To partially conclude, philosophy does not only aim at "what" is not given a priori and not authorised because under control. It also aims at activating an intellectual and radical operation which would take the inquiry about "culture" and "identity" away from the fabrication of externally imposed, and malignantly tabooed, ascriptions. Since a few prominent scholars of social sciences are today in struggle for realigning the viewer with the viewed, the coloniers with the colonised, and the powerful with the powerless, the central aim of philosophy remains timelessly the same: turning the realm of thoughtlessness and distractedness into a place of confrontation.

PART I: GENESIS, MATERIALISATION, BOUNDARIES, AND MEANINGS OF "MINORITY" AS SUBALTERN OTHERNESS

"The excluded are not simply included into the community.
Rather, their inclusion disrupts the very notion of stable community.
Traditionally, democracy does not create freedom among equals,
as it often hoped. It is a rather divisive political system
involving those who possess the status in the political community
and those who do not."

Jacques Rancière,
On the Shores of Politics (1994)

CHAPTER ONE
Setting the Scene

As stated in the introduction, a philosophical investigation over minority communities, or, more properly, over subaltern groups, would serve first and foremost to disentangle the terminological carrier of "culture" and "identity" in the field of social sciences. Both, whereby applied over the notion of "community", have been a scholarly source of confrontation and turned into a scholarly battleground due to the various issues of pedigree dilemma. It followed that the instrumental use of the category of "cultural identity" has largely become the property of groups despite its high level of ambiguity and vagueness. The failure of defining any substance of "cultural identity" lies in the definition itself, thus in the naming and defining any community. The latter, which is clearly a political action (Marchart 2018: 160-163), is not only an attempt to theoretically frame but also to epistemologically possess the substance of one's group essence in relation to complex power structures that do not always refer to one single place.

Nevertheless, the tandem identity-and-culture has been central for a much-discussed and often neglected debate underlining a large variety of political phenomena. Categories of "identity" and "culture" alike highlight a twofold manifestation of the field of so-called "identity politics" in the light of the return of history and the denial of the opinion which assured the end. In this regard, "identity" has always been a never-ending discussion in the circle of philosophy since Parmenides's time, while, conversely, "culture" has recently joined the run. To put it simply, the category of culture has been presented as a play of differences (Spivak 1999: 356), one of the most successful regulators for setting up modalities of knowing what is different. The ethnicity-based category of identity has generally met resistance in the legal doctrine and beyond, since it is often in tension with a too culturalist interpretation of identity signifiers. As a matter of fact, an investigation of "culture" through the prism of ethnicity has repeatedly led to uncertainty and left space for ethno-politicist discourse to satisfy certain interests (Hall 2008: 33).

However, it would not be possible to imagine the sphere of politics entirely disconnected from both terms. Social scientists have repeatedly referred to the category of identity along with that of culture as a binarism that manifests itself by unfolding and thereby displaying all facets of peoplehood and how its performativity within a specific realm is rendered meaningful.

Here, the lack of a shared scholarly definition of both terms continues to refrain scholars from coming up with a standardised and recognised definition. Some offer multiple definitions that vary among a large number of single terms, while, conversely, others tend to conflate two or more terms by using them at the same time, thereby without clarifying one of the most basic but problematic and controversial issues in the philosophy circle. Within this, particular attention has been drawn to those modalities and practices by which cultural claims and collective identities are transmitted into the wider public, narrowing down the focus of the investigation into the realm of everyday life and how identity performativity is made meaningful in the realm of everydayness.

Although such widespread approach has gained popularity in social sciences, minority issues have continuously been investigated within the field of "identity politics". The latter is of fairly recent provenance in the field of identity and culture. There would be no longer problems with ethno-politics in theory if and only if ethnopolitics would not have become an extremely problematic and highly controversial terrain where interpretations and assertions of many kinds are malignantly made (Fukuyama 2018). Relatedly, many point out how a wide range of minority groups have only benefitted from their "status" by peculiarly abusing issues of diversity for their own purposes, and how social sciences often end up in paradoxical, contradictory circumstances in their attempt to rightly tackle their social demands and cultural claims. In political terms, for example, Fukuyama has recently argued that in the West the Liberal Left has focussed less on promoting equality and interests of the society as a whole, campaigning instead for a variety of specific groups perceived as subaltern and not yet fully recognised — such as blacks, immigrants, women, LGBTQI+ communities, refugees, and the like. In contrast, the Liberal Right has recently begun to (re-)define itself along a patriotic or radical form of nationalism in order to seek out protection of traditional and pristine forms of national identities that are often explicitly connected to a radical, and too trivial, interpretation of race, belonging, religion, and so forth (2018: 7).

In CEE, most academic works and studies have identified minority groups through an old-fashioned use of the term "ethnos", whose cultural affiliation lies in the literal translation of the Greek "ethnos" (ἔθνος) —namely, a "people". By doing so, social sciences and related traditional approaches have so far gained very little in conceiving what identities really are: a complex of articulated collective wills. In their continuous attempts to define peoplehood, the dominant tendency is still to view, designate, and categorise groups in general, and minorities in particular, along ethnic lines by encompassing intersectional facets of religion and race. This oversimplified perspective of peoplehood labels a "minority" as a compact entity and unitary actor to be at best used for transient analysis and looked at for further stabilisation of interethnic dimensions of the political everyday. In the meantime, however, the rise of newly arrived minorities seeking out recognition along different lines from those social sciences were accustomed to, and within specific segments of a peoplehood (e.g., gender and different lifestyle), have definitely opened up the door to new challenging paradigms. If one should also consider the large number of intersectional aspects in (co-)existing groups within a people, ethnos itself is not purely ethnos anymore. Thus, the latter risks counter-legitimisation in theory and misleading interpretations of the issues at stake.

Against this pitfall, it seems much more central to deepen spatio-temporal structures and agencies of peoplehood by navigating within and in between a vast array of facets that a given minority might own and project while coming into being or becoming another. Since there is no longer a natural or standard yardstick by which scholars measure facets of peoplehood, it is surely worth investigating from within the subject-matter rather than externally imposing a set of features and ascriptions upon it. Hence, the main aim is not only understanding the logic of circumstances under which a minority group becomes aware of one's own neglected or deprived status. It is not even only related to a minority's attempt to go beyond or benefit from its own status of subordination. It is rather a philosophical attempt to unravel stereotypes and disentangle power conjectures that processes of othering interwove epistemologically in circumstances under which impulses of cultural and political forces emerge and come into being.

In the attempt to address both constitution(s) and dissolution(s) of minority identities in space and time, shedding light on a (post-Communist) human condition among minority members would be better described along the transformation of power and the fabrication of subordination among those who have historically coped with emergences, social inequalities, dismantlement of social ties of reciprocity, acceptance of survival habitus. Perhaps not entirely an ex-colonial territory such as those geographically located in the Global

South (e.g., Latin America, Africa, Southeast Asia), the post-Communist CEE as a whole could be understood as a post-colonial region in a sense that it is connected with the critique of Western modernity discussed largely in postcolonial studies, if the latter is, of course, understood in terms of critical thinking (Kołodziejczyk 2010: 135).

To the extent that group identity is solely treated along the freestanding and ethnos-centred paradigm of "cultural identity", a variety of voiceless individuals and hidden communities will be firmly denied from their circle of humanity (Gramsci 1971). Therefore, such a philosophical approach shall here avoid the above-mentioned use of rigid and old-fashioned literature along with questions on the variety of constantly weighed, and timely redefined, normative implications of minority groups. In doing so, this study critically deals with an always-present reference to the carrier of "identity" and "culture" in its objective source of instability and conflicts that have been employed in literature so far, thereby rejecting externally imposed ascriptions of heathenness, paganism, and savageness, collective exoticism and inferiority. Without any doubt, this study is not an exclusive place to resolve such a serious issue completely. It may, however, come in support to the subject-matter at stake after a long period of apparent calm, whose aftermaths have seen identity and culture alike becoming the favourite objects for "political entrepreneurs". By doing so, they have benefitted from, and seized power positions, by frivolously campaigning for stabilisation and potential achievement of full-fledged democracy standards in the post-1989 transition period.

As time has passed by, minority issues have been rapidly used to mobilise nationalistic rhetoric and campaigns to reinforce old-fashioned and a priori ethnic-defined traits. Here, although it seems that we cannot escape from thinking about politics in general and ourselves in particular in identity terms, Spivak's criticism on culture and identity reveals that both notions, per se granted and given, or externally constructed, do not, and will not, cut much ice (1999: 354). In fact, the application of both terms over specific segments of the population in order to depict a group—no matter whether a community or a minority—would extremely blur the ongoing investigation. According to Didi-Huberman's position, the nonexistence of a people, of an ethnos as qua people and its constitutive ideological instrument of division, gives more credits to the existence of coexistent peoples, not from one population to another, but even within the same people—with the mental or social interior of it—no matter how coherent we would like to imagine it to be, which is, moreover, never the case (2016: 66). However, whether such idea of coexistence has been hypostasized into the generality of people's own identity by Marxist scholarship among others, in the post-Communist CEE ideological hypostatisation or generalisation of peoplehood—no matter how diverse it was from within—has to be legitimised by the contingency of post-1989 events. Since then, the ideological imposition of universalism and egalitarianism has marked a binary along which philosophical interpretation of peoplehood has never ceased to influence the cultural debate over group identities. The idea of the so-called (post-)homo sovieticus and others alike, fades away from one's great working class that even (neo-)Marxists stopped adopting despite the idea of one's humanity distributed along economic factors and divided because of them into people-classes. Interestingly enough, (neo-)liberal universalists and egalitarianists have similarly understood humanity as one, but distributed into people-nations and divided just because of them. Beyond misleading picture in the post-Communist political spectrum, both approaches overlook what Didi-Huberman calls mental or social interior differences of the same population—namely, a different angle of investigation that shifted radically from the debate on the "essence versus construct" dilemma (Makariev 2017) with regards to whether a given community acquaintances one's identity throughout a period of contingent (re)construction, or essentially received it as timeless pre-given feature. Therefore, further use of the term "minority" does not have the purpose of replacing the philosophical concept of "subaltern". Yet, it only aims at (a) maintaining the topic of this investigation centred; (b) keeping a constant focus on the specificity of the subject-matter of this monograph; and (c) criticising the categorisation and standardisation of the term itself. By doing so, the conceptualisation of "identity building" with regards to minority groups in the post-Communist Europe shall be philosophically employed to set the scene for a critical investigation through which dichotomy of opinions between essentialists (also well-known as "primordialists") and constructivists will move critically beyond.

It follows that effort for such philosophical investigation shall be first and foremost oriented to destabilise the centre-periphery along the majority-minority dualism. It shall also dismantle the constructive majoritarian "process of othering" as well as minority's "becoming another", thereby striving for the recovery of the subjugated societal position of occluded marginal groups—either ethnic minorities or subaltern subjects. By focusing more on the interplay between the structure and its agency to seek out factors and circumstances, the attention is also shifted to the marginalised and invisible, those without a name, without papers, without lodging, without rights, and without images.

CHAPTER TWO

Minority Identities in Central and Eastern Europe: A Critical Overview

The aftermath of the Communist period brought the academic world to deal with minority issues through three different scholarships in the field of social sciences. The first one, so-called essentialism, has always sustained the determination of communitarian identities along pure and pristine forms of indigenousness and belongingness, which are shaped into basic group identity (Isaacs 1975: 38). Moreover, for essentialists characters of identity have a pre-given, biological, cultural, and historical dimension which reflect *an* identity and its pre-conditional links of belonging. In general, they separate an identity from others due to cultural diversities that are diversities from birth (Viola 2008: 524). According to the twofold category of "cultural identity", a people has not chosen its own identity since the latter is an expression of thinking which refers to an association of identity and authenticity (Makariev 2017). This is not so different, after all, from what Heidegger's comments on Parmenides's fragments have argued. In contemporary identity-contested societies, however, search for definition for what identity really is has increasingly blurred an already much-discussed subject of discussion whose aim seems to ground the high level of diversity between one group and another rather than looking for similarities for coexistence. In this regard, it is no longer possible to handle issues of communitarian identities through the philosophical tautology that Martin Heidegger's 'Beyng' referred to—namely, the proportion of "A is equal to A" (A = A). The eventual play of difference-as-difference has traditionally referred to the concept of "sameness", thereby implying a relation of "with" playing the role of a mediator, a connection, a synthesis, a unification into a unity. The latter, however, renders more obscure Parmenides's enigmatic fragment (τό αὐτό), whereby thinking and Being belong together in the Same and by virtue of this Same. (Heidegger 1969: 25–27). To put it simply, here, identity belongs to a being, and vice versa. Whether such an approach would have had a central role throughout the national-buildings of the post-Communist Eastern Bloc's nations, many point out that the latter is no longer influential across the region. According to the subject-matter of this study, it is not particularly so with regards to sub-national groups which do not identify themselves with majoritarian cultural sameness. Therefore, identity is, by definition, pre-given and not supposed to change or to vary much within a group. In reference to the notion of culture, a given-at-birth identity stems from the "givens", or, more precisely, from inevitably assumed givers of social existence (Benhabib 2002: 50–55). The main risk to consider here is that of counting both majoritarian cultural systems and minority identities anachronistically and a-historically, taking them for granted and in the way they are, thinking that they have always been as such over time, biasing an overall association of peoplehood with reference to either a religious belief system (Abeysekara 2011) or to a supposedly inherited paternal and maternal form of genetics. No matter under which circumstances identity grows intensively in support of its culture, in its turn the latter represents a set of living values and performance around which people rally, gather, and become aware of their own "we". It would seem that this form of "we-ness" is first and foremost a self-constituting and self-designing action that seeks to secure a movement of gathering, which may be durational or imply occasional, periodic, or bodily mobilising group identity. Referring to such collective "we-ness" means to refer to a group action that is prompt to perform it. In few words, "we-ness" constitutes a movement in space and time to let this "we" happen and constitute itself, preceding any specific demand of equality and justice (Butler 2016: 56–58).

From this viewpoint, the CEE has a long tradition of a variety of protests and breakaway movements rejecting, opposing and disentangling imposed societal sameness. Against Communism, for example, under which ethno-national majoritarian cultural systems came out after remaining trapped in a prison-style waiting room since the end of the WWII, that moment of political reactivation mobilised unrecognised collectives by turning themselves into counter-hegemony entities, which, on the one hand, activated their subalternity, and, on the other hand, set others apart due to the inevitable function of becoming hegemony. This twofold movement of "We-ness" was visible in the Czech-Slovak conflictual relations during the Communist time (McDermott and Pinerová 2015). Especially in the period of Antonín Novotný's leadership and his "Praguecentrism", the national sentiment of the Slovak counterpart was moved upward to political emancipation organised around a renewal of religious life and church activities (2015: 115). Similarly, the not yet resolved interethnic tensions between Romanians and Hungarians in the contested region of Transylvania are instructive to affirm how ethno-national identities were mixed with elements of Communist ideology (Goina 2015: 137), on the one hand, yet remaining central points of cultural reference under the parapet of the Moscow-oriented Communist ideology, on the other.

In 1985, perhaps the most explicit philosophical contribution ever made, Milan Kundera began to gain popularity in the West even prior to the definite demise of the Soviet Union and its politically aligned satellite region. In his *The Tragedy of Central Europe* (1985) he noticed how the Communist experience had tragically driven Central European populations' identity away from their own being, beyond their own historical destiny of civilisation, forcing the region itself to lose its real identity. Kundera culturally addressed those inconspicuous, albeit vivid under the parapet of Communist ideology and institutional structures, national identities as a ready-made set of endowments and identifications that every group shares at a given time and space. In other words, Kundera understood sub-Communist national identities as stable, and pre-determined, depending on one's European identity. This wide range of national identities was found into a subaltern minority position in their own space of existence, put at risk of losing their own Western influence.

Therefore, although a philosophical enquiry over the category of identity has been subject of contestation since the time of Parmenides, the latter has been polarised since the 1950s. After the proposals of the psychologist Erick Erickson, identity has arrived in the views of cultural politics and group dynamics during the 1980s and 1990s. In fact, it would seem that Kundera's depiction of the Central European tragedy follows up the academic contributions of Shils (1957), Geerts (1963), and Isaac (1975), with whom the Czech philosopher would have been probably familiar with, and influenced by. In this, the change of cultural contexts and spatio-temporal transformation that the Central European identity went through, could not allow Soviet Republics to endure over time. Against this, it would seem that Kundera opposed CEE's elements of history and origins, nationalities, and other affiliations to, or alignment with, linguistic as well as religious facets and geopolitical topography whose distinctive features, happened to be even before they would take the risk to face the last stage of meaningfulness.

Hence, traditional methodologies of the social sciences predispose scholars to take an essentialist approach over issues related to group identities. It comes, perhaps as natural, to strive to the exploration of what lies beyond the "surface" — namely, beyond what is visible, and reveal the essence of the object under investigation (Makariev 2017). After all, this is what Kundera referred to in his description of oppressed national (minority) identities and repressed cultures that Ukrainians, Belarusians, Armenians, Latvians, Lithuanians, and many others, kept alive by struggling to survive against the foreign, uniform, standardising, centralising, determined empire of "a single Russian people", or, as was more commonly expressed in that age of generalised verbal mystification, of a "single Soviet people". To a certain extent, Kundera unravelled how vividly the Central European defence of its national identities occurred against an externally imposed and ideologically constructed identity of the detested Communist cultural policy. However, he overlooked the different nuances that those sub-national entities had from within. It came exclusively to point out how the essence of Central Europe's different national identities found themselves under fire and away from their Western-ness.

To a certain extent, Kundera's quasi-essentialist critique was opposed to the deeply a-national, antinational, supranational Communist identity, which was aimed at reconstructing Central European identity by keeping the region away from its cultural home and thereby ceasing a perception of cultural unity of Europe as a whole. Hence, one could state that such dichotomy of Eastern identities along the Western-Eastern axis has surmounted along cultural lines and reflected hidden division of Europe itself. While Western scholars have perceived identity in consideration of a hybrid and multiple being (Ha 2008: 64), others in Eastern Europe regard it as a sense of belonging. Reflecting on Kundera's cultural parallelism over such division of Western Europe and the Communist orbit, the notion of identity seems nowadays to have gone beyond its old-fashioned geographical reference of locality and definitely become much more than that, as Kundera himself had pointed out. Indeed, Europe as a cultural whole is currently shaping a mental construct (Glavanakova 2016: 13) onto which one might perhaps be in agreement with or have sympathy for. It might be also possible to support Europe as a whole without necessarily projecting a banally historicised struggle of cultural identities in the attempt to keep its ethno-national uniqueness alive. It might instead respect identities without forced assimilations. For example, conservatives have always kept arguing about the fact that cultures should be preserved in order to maintain a respectable degree of differences among them. Decades onwards what Kundera retained a large number of authenticities with regards to those national identities closed-off and encapsulated into assimilating prison-style larger nations, the post-1989 nation-buildings have come to instrumentally impose a separation among European regions. Veiled by controversial practices of protection from threats of cultural hybridity and accepted for guaranteeing security against conflict and instability (Benhabib 2002), what the overwhelmingly detested Communist policy did against those national minorities is what post-Communist European socio-cultural majority systems perpetuate against minority groups and their cultures.

In post-Communist societies and their current processes of identity transformation, which are centrally paramount to critically understand minority issues in CEE, essentialist argumentations face challenges of contingent circumstances related to time and space. As a matter of fact, human beings have to be considered in the particular condition in which they happen to be (Viola 2008: 525), such as the issue of Balkan Muslims or Roma communities. In turn, it may logically follow the critical statement that group identities have been neither exclusively atomised nor ahistorical nor fixed. On the contrary, they have changed and developed themselves through time, and they will continue to (Cheskin 2016). Here, power of contingency becomes even clearer when understood through the prism of a structuralist approach. The latter has a long story in social science and particularly in social philosophy, of who (e.g., individual or collective actions and behaviour) or, alternatively, of how (e.g., external, pre-existing, wider institutional, social, cultural structures) structural change can be driven and people can be (re)shaped along with their social behaviour (Schwandner-Sievers 2019: 22). Because of this, structuralism can be referred as "circumstantialism" in accordance with Sehila Benhabib's approach (2002).

Against the essentialist pitfall, circumstantialism tackles all identity-related issues by claiming that nodal points around which identity and culture are constructed, and construct themselves, are necessarily dynamic, flowing, self-conflicting, and inconsistent. In simpler words, such scholarship avoids the mistake of "essentialising", namely – of thinking that each culture has a unique and homogenous essence that all its members uniformly share (Baggini 2018: xxi).

Therefore, identity and culture are constantly being timed because time itself influences or produces identities (Irwin 2000) within a space which, either understood as a physical location or as an imaginary locum, defines identity itself. In the same vein, "identity" does not denote anything that remains static and unchanging through history; unlike what essentialist scholars sustain, it neither excludes nor dismisses the probability to be at risk, exposed to, or stimulated for, a potential development, transformation, or complete change. Under certain circumstances, which may change anytime, a group identity may change accordingly, and it does indeed develop or transform itself. Even in cases when members belonging to a community consider themselves "the same", their "sameness" cannot stand the almost certain differences from within, such as modes of thinking and living and socio-economic background, separated by an infinite number of other differences (Cheskin 2016: 32). Within this heterogeneous context, spatiality along with temporality (and ethicality) are analytical lenses that compose a key-relation for all group identities and bring out the political substance of each (re)construction (Hansen 2006, quoted in Zambelli 2008: 3).

Because of this, constructivists argue that a given group identity is not a stably a-historical entity. It is instead the result of a symbolic construction that continues to maintain timely a series of constructed boundaries reflecting itself to/against an "other" or more than one pole/point of reference (Barth 1969). Among others, it may affirm that symbols play a paramount role in triggering certain mental operations whose functions begin in a social framework within which memories, in terms of collective action activity of recollection, shape notable storing, generalising, and sharing (Kushnir 2017: 7). On the one hand, the "essentialist question" might arise here by highlighting that—no matter what circumstances—any result of change and transformation happens to begin from a "static being". In fact, following this approach, one would point out that prior to becoming something other than it was at the very beginning, *an* identity has had a stable identity at least once, along with its cultural elements that embodied it. On the other hand, however, it would not only seem herculean to go back to the roots and affirm certain paraphernalia of pure indigenousness or belonging. In fact, the more we zoom into the past, the more the ancestral history of our being begins to overlap with that of everyone else on the planet, there cannot be *a* society or *an* identity which owns the final measuring rod. It is not only admittedly problematic to attempt to isolate a given group from another in search of such pristineness, but it is also futile to think about pure racial, ethnic or national signifiers since they are just ephemeral and not what we imagine them to be when we look upon them from the deep past in accordance with the culture we have and with the politics we have (Saini 2019: 180). It is also not plausible to attempt to rule out that an a priori reduction, minimisation, or *tout court* exclusion from encounters between one identity and another will avoid risks of destruction, or secure survival and existence over time, exclusion to power transformation (Habermas 1998 mentioned in Matustik 1993: 34). Even those circumstances where meanings or concepts of a group identity have become sedimentary over time, contingent transformation of power do not make them any more real or less subjected to further transformations. It is simply the case in which community members have naturalised themselves into a particular group (Laclau 1990: 34). As a matter of fact, a given group's "cultural identity" might have been kept isolated over time just for the sake of being protected from external interactions and spatio-temporal changes. However, all of these do not exclude that such "cultural identity" will lead itself to become other than it was before, avoiding to become a museum piece (Waligore 2009: 33). And even under these circumstances, forms of cultural isolation cannot guarantee no one's identity to be secured and away from the risk of death due to the destructive radical happenings that natural disasters, genocide or extinction might manifest.

To come thus to a partial conclusion, one could here affirm that if identities were unitary, fixed, and immutable, they could not be nowadays subject to contestation (Norton 2000: 127). In light of spatial changes and variations in time across the world, it is quite impossible to sustain some kinds of essentialist claims over cultural identities and communities. At the same time, however, similar to issues that essentialist scholars deal with, contingency might undermine group dynamics and self-conflicting spatiotemporal circumstances by depicting a given identity as inconsistent. A minority perspective offers here an important angle of investigation regardless of contingent circumstances which group identities are subjected to. It seems difficult to completely discredit, or take easily for granted, that identity's change, as well as development and transformations, happen inconsistently. The entire CEE is the appropriate region where minority identities have been either formed or constructed from scratch or developed in the attempt to encourage ambitious narratives, including autonomy and projects for full self-government (Pentassuglia 2018: 292). In the last decades, there have been many examples of peoples embodying themselves into a process of becoming by forming a way of speech, demanding a change in policy, or attempting to dissolve a government (Butler 2016:49) or any other form of power. This is, after all, the recent historical path that in the former Eastern bloc many groups of people have gone through, transforming or/and adapting themselves into a socio-political realm instead of another to come. In more philosophical terms, it is the reversal of the relationship of forces (Foucault 1977: 154), whereby once a minority group declares a context in which it lives as completely different from the one in which it was adopted before, and it destroys the inertia of the status quo by representing a group of people and making itself the body of a new assembling (Badiou 2016), such process of becoming happens thanks to a conscious unbecoming. In this regard, we must go beyond the numerical understanding of "becoming other". In other words, it is a transformation and identity negotiation – especially in those turning themselves into a minority position – that have little to do with becoming, thus seeking out, a numerical majority. It is rather aimed at activating a process that encapsulates not the more individuals of a population into a symbolic one (Marchart 2018).

Given this token, the recent literature dealing with the definition of cultural identity has largely moved away from any attempt of "essentialisation" of collective identities by turning more and more to a "circumstantialist" approach. The latter offers another straightforward and prominent approach to the burning question of identity and group cultures. Away from falling into the pitfall of essentialising, circumstantialism is often employed to look underneath what really a given group identity seems to be while attempting to identify contingencies and circumstances in order to venture the parapet of externally constructed essences upon a certain identity rather than another.

Richard Mole, among others, has provided an account of how social agents identifying with numerous categorical forms of identity might be expected to alter identity's actions depending on the context. For example, the Armenian notion of *hayadardzutyun*, which can be literally translated as "back to the roots", refers to the attempt of awakening a new kind of Armenian solidarity towards those "forgotten Armenian fellows" who settled down all over the world after being scattered in the aftermaths of the "1915 Genocide". While *hayadardzutyun* would seem to proudly keep an ahistorical "we-ness" to demonstrate how the "Armenian being" has not been eroded, the latter tends (purposefully?) to overlook different forms of either being or feeling Armenian. As a matter of historical facts, the so-called "Armenian-ness"[1] does not represent two distinct identities but a plurality of forms of "being Armenian" throughout history (Bakalian 1993). In this regards, what would seem to potentially be recalled a contemporary "Armenian Zionism", it is instead a politics-driven revival campaign of historical upheavals that Armenian communities have passed through. Without any doubt, endurance has historically been the Armenian legacy (Goldenberg 1994: 133) since the small Caucasian nation has always tried to revitalise the third and fourth diaspora-born generation of Armenian descendants whose reference to Armenian-ness has little to do with that of Armenia-based peers.

Interestingly enough, this case study might point critically out how essentialism of Armenian culture as well as the analysis of structures

---

[1] The article 19 of the Armenian constitution recognises the term Armenian-ness as the identity of Armenians and its millenarian heritage.

within which different forms of Armenian-ness have been formed to comprehend identity's real substance of Armenian people in complete dependency on historical contingencies and social circumstances, how structures themselves are able to trigger identity's (re-)actions (Mole 2007, cited by Dawson 2014: 63). Of particular interest is that such paradigm seems to highlight essentialist attitudes of both scholarship, essentialism, as well as constructivism. To a certain extent, in fact, the main argumentation cannot be concerned with the fact that Armenians have not lost their identity of being a sort of community, whereas that they have held onto it and transformed it throughout historical contingencies (Bakalian 1993). Therefore, a focus on circumstances tends to highlight how processes of othering or association with one object or concept rather than another, are familiar to any community.

From a historical perspective, minority identities in CEE have always been dependent on processes of becoming due to being subjected to externally imposed changes. From the fate of national minorities under Communist experience (Fejtö 1974) to minority state of affairs in post-Communist democracies, transformations of group identities have been historically designated in the form of minority and subaltern position. Hiding from ethnic cleansing, surviving from wartime mass deportations, resisting patriarchy-oriented traditional peer-pressure in the private and public sphere, or adapting themselves to newly imposed constructed collective identities, minority groups have consciously transformed themselves in the attempt to become something different than they were in the previous circumstances (Badiou 2016: 27). Either for surviving in new socio-political realms or destroying their own previous inertia (e.g. status quo) in order to secure themselves in a different body than the precedent one, all of these examples point out how each communitarian identity has been timed into a space throughout a "minority becoming"[2] that co-happened with an ethological (trans-)/formation of networked relations (Madhu 2014). Of particular interest is the potential refusal to be substantially "taken in" by the available cultural-political option of whatever reasons throughout a process of "minority becoming". This largely refers to what Gilles Deleuze and Félix Guattari have formulated through the prism of the macro-political arena, suggesting to "becoming-minor" in order to begin with a further process of universalisation (1986). The latter is nothing but a process of de-grounding from a previous space of existence. In other

---

[2] From now on, this philosophical concept refers to Prabakaran Madhu's response to Sundar Sarukai's PN Shameer Memorial lecture on "Becoming Minority" delivered at the History Department of the Sri Shankara University for Sanskrit at Kalady (India) on April 24, 2015; retrieved from https://www.academia.edu/12143886/Becoming_Minority on January 22, 2018.

words, more specifically in Badiou's language, this process reveals a "minority detachment" from the status quo which is initiated by declaring itself "a people". Therefore, this action is quite performative since it is for a new collective being. One might also notice how along the road toward becoming an "Other", thus detached from those who were once "one's own", there might be the "opportunity of the half-way" to be distinguished as a well-informed outsider (Chomsky 1999: 22). Following such philosophically collected viewpoint, which is mainly based on Deleuze and Guattari's "becoming-minor", the process of "minority becoming" anticipates the momentum of minority detachment and declaration, and displays a large number of intra-group dynamics. For instance, a post-Communist reading of the demise of the Socialist society demonstrates how the process of becoming is a radical rupture from the previous space of existence. Within this, a given (minority) identity was used to adapt itself for de-grounding, thereby displaying the pre-emerging conditionality of "becoming-minor". At the same time, what is a "minority becoming" unfolds itself by shaping a consciously transformative movement. It is, in other words, a conscious – and not externally imposed – dislocation, namely - a radical rupture that may lead in the direction of an unknown, unsecured, or challenging pathway, yet directed through a desire of being toward the universal. Among others, Laclau recalls the local case of the Polish trade union movement "Solidarność" (e.g. solidarity) whose initial articulation was very particular and directed to the Gdansk dock workers, but it managed to activate its hidden potential of "becoming-major" – namely, the ability to achieve the status of full universality (Marchart 2018: 136).

In other words, on the one hand, this becoming-minor is a contingent and eventual transformation (Madhu 2014), that is, an antithesis as well as a negation of the essentialist, common understanding of identity as a pre-given, stationary or static being. On the other hand, it stands in contrast to the inconsistency of identity formation that might trap constructivists. Minority groups have historically shown how to consciously trigger a process of becoming something they were not before, detaching themselves from the previous clearly demarked conditions of a space that they ceased to recognise as their own. For instance, the climate of violence, humiliation, deportation, and persecution that since the collapse of the Ottoman Empire up until the 1980s coerced the Christian minority of Ottoman and Turkish Armenians to consciously convert to Islam in order to hide and survive. Armenians were aware that disclosing their identity would have exposed them to risks. Throughout, Turkey's ethnic Armenians no longer saw themselves as Armenians. In the eyes of the Turkish population Armenians became *dönmes* (literally "converts" in the Turkish language), trapped in between double discrimination by Armenia-based Armenian peers who ceased to recognise them as such, and by Turks for whom they were visibly converts only to survive (Hadjian 2018). Similarly, the ethnic Albanian population shows nowadays how contingencies of historical events can trigger the process of *becoming other*.

In general, any process of becoming shows how each group (minority) identity may effectively unfold itself by freeing and thereby disentangling a given community from those spatio-temporal circumstances it was in. In particular, it can also create from scratch conditions for adaption into a new realm, paving the way to further debate on how "becoming a minority" can also be seen as a conscious act of suspending a self-identification in space and time and setting the stage for an existential event that breaks away from the previous contingencies and moves forward. In this regard, while Ernesto Laclau radically sustains that a group's action of becoming has to be understood as unwinding, namely, a claim of freedom which is reversal (2000: 55), Soldado, too, affirms that the process of becoming requires a change of identity which may potentially cross frontiers, it definitely becomes an "ex", a "former" from that time and space which no longer exist but represent the "ex", the "former" (2019: 11). For this reason, Lauclau argues that there are not just identities but, rather, identification (2000) that can be constructed through the equivalence of a plurality of elements. Despite the fact that such "required identification" brings light at the heart of the basic ambiguities of all identities, circumstantialist scholarship claims that the formation of a meaningful group identity is almost impossible without some reference to an external and an "other" group, subject, symbol, discourse, and so forth.

As mentioned above, a group identity can happen to come into being through an association of one object or one concept. Moreover, such identification may take place along with a reference to a space and specific period of time. This dialectical, mutual process of self-understanding and becoming raises the unavoidable question of otherness. The latter, which is a philosophical category to refer to, does not reallot a dynamic, relative, and conditionally dependent reflection between the collective Self and the foreign "Other" due to a ceaselessly fluctuating movement. It is rather a mutual, contingent association of a people's identity with itself, modelling some differences with a respective other in order to perceive a certain distance in between, with whom it is (not) sharing a common set of attributes, tastes, appearances, and so forth. This process of othering, which is centrally paramount in constructing a social identity, is therefore about associating the Self with an object among others, or with a concept among others. Thus, identity is here seen as a range along a spectrum of choices rather than a static, pre-given quality. Once again, the identity of the Armenian dönmes stemmed from a consciously-taken decision to suspend their previous identity and accept another with the attempt to avoid being recognised as gâvur, namely – "infidels", during the collapse of the Ottoman Empire and the parallel escalation of violence that targeted ethnic Armenians and other Christian minorities. By assuming an Other's identity, which, paradoxically, represented one of their persecutors, they refused to keep their family name's suffix "-yan", which continues nowadays to identify the ethnic Armenian belonging. The loss of such signifier of communitarian identity was not the worst thing to happen to Ottoman Armenians since their first contingent need was for the body to be alive (Hadjian 2018). Similar to the process of "minority becoming", this act of othering may also occur by movement. It is, in other words, a constant association with time and space that many come to be put at stake: changing the ground or a historical situation in which the image of the respective other is about to change as well. Once again, Armenians are perhaps the most scattered community across the world due to historical upheavals they have been exposed to. They would be found in almost the entire universe of possibilities: those based in Armenia, those from Diaspora communities, those from one country who emigrated to another, and those from Turkey, the majority of whom claims to have survived under the Armenian sun but instead shows a certain affiliation to Islam nowadays. Another similar case recalls the dissolution of the Soviet Bloc and its satellite region, in which the rise of national identities has shown how a process of "minority becoming" is parallel to "othering majority", constructed within socio-cultural boundaries around which it is decided who is in (intergroup solidarity) and who is out (outgroup dynamics of exclusion).

Once again, a "minority perspective" here has to be employed. Indeed, it more likely suggests that overlooking individuals' as well as particular communities' desire of choosing and thereby consciously constructing by themselves between/among various overlapping nodal points, around which they decide to be aligned with, in potential accordance with specific or more general aspects of political, economic, and social preferences, geographical locations, ethnic and racial backgrounds, family and national histories, genders, and country's name printed in official documents (e.g., ID, passport, security documents), is wrong. In fact, a process of "becoming-minor" or "other" has nothing to do, or perhaps very little, with the sociological or anthropological processes of self-ghettoisation. It could be indeed plausible to claim that the transformation of a given community happens either due to an externally imposed force that forces its members to become something they are not, or due to a collectively internal decision that begins to transform the community from within. For instance, an externally imposed construction of identity (e.g., social stigma, see Goffman) often neglects the idea that such identity may critically depend on the claims which members can make in different contexts (e.g., space) and at different times (e.g., historical epochs and timely contingent experiences). The process of "minority becoming" unfolds itself through a one-sided understanding of the Self, either personally or collectively, and reflecting an "Other" in turn for coming to being. The "Other" performs thus a structural role, haunting the subject for whom the Other is a necessary self-representation albeit by negation (Glavanakova 2016: 12). In this case, a minority perspective suggests that a group identity is *from below* consolidated if and only if the in-group's identity (Self) is contrasted to a rival out-group's one (Cheskin 2016: 150). This so called "constitutive other" has negatively followed exclusionary or "positively discriminatory" (Mouffe and Laclau 1985) paths of constitution. However, constitution of an "other" aimed at unravelling a process of becoming had not positively paid off to minority groups which have been primarily subjected to segregation. "Otherness" plays in the arena of sociocultural differences, which is turned into an open form of marginalisation, exclusion, and hostility (Gržinić 2019:183). For example, while the Communist experience in CEE brought a large number of peoples to be part of an "identity project" on behalf of the "Great Proletariat", in the post-1989 era minority identities have been at first constructed and liable to manipulation by external agents from the majoritarian cultural system. Secondly, they have been stimulated to such difference by internal actors (Craib 1998). Because of this, it is even clearer that this philosophical investigation over identity has to refer to the issue of identification, that is, in a few words, how an individual, or a specific group, poses itself in relation to another individual or group, which in turn does the same, occupying yet another position in the social realm (Cheskin 2016: 29). To reiterate the Polish example of Solidarność, the latter initially functioned as a slogan of a local group of workers – namely, a signifier for a particular demand into a particular context. Only later on, it began to represent a name of and for the opposition as such for an alternative system of diversity across the region (Marchart 2018: 162).

Perhaps, the fundamental and most complicated problem is here to determine which contextual factor, and under what occasion (e.g. circumstance), plays a role in the initial paradox of positioning in time and space (Naumović 2002: 15). In this regard, a minority group does not only compromise its socio-cultural identity according to "what it thinks to be", but it also acts in order to "coming into being" by activating its "hidden constitutive other" and thereby gaining a historical and spatial awareness of what the community is and what the others are, and, in its turn, of its collective Self and its "Other within" (Jenkins 1996: 5). This generally stresses differences rather than similarities. However, it is important to note how identity constructions have not been driven by a moral force for equally representing the Self and the Other in their differences. Conversely, in post-Communist Europe and beyond "identity projects" have included so far socio-political strategies for the construction of the Self through a representation of the Other as an existential threat, as inferior, as an upcoming violation of universal principles, as simply different.

However, if othering becomes necessary for an act of liberation, the former requires also a series of several displacements as a *conditio sine qua non*. Such conditionality of displacement, which occurs inevitably along the lines of differences, has so far undergone a considerable process of inflation in contemporary thought (Laclau 2016: 76) as one of the most explanatory paradigms to employ. Without any doubt, the contemporary phenomenon of populism has politically affirmed itself as one of the biggest, and culturally successful, processes of "othering" against the alien. It has particularly embedded a style of speaking that addresses itself directly to the people, going beyond its representatives and notables by using an identitary rhetoric that expresses fear and rejection of the alien. Although processes of othering, whenever found, imply the (re-)construction of the Self accordingly, populism is nowadays managing to construct and draw an image of a certain people based on antagonistic features of a segment of society, certain (in)capacities, land and blood, and so on. It constructively merges one's idea of democratic, acceptable people with that of danger, uncertainty, and perilous masses (Rancière 2016: 101). This excludes processes of othering from any definition of an either political or cultural phenomenon. To a certain extent, it started to be rooted a couple of decades ago in the academic work of Laclau and Mouffle (1985) pertaining to the so-called "logic of equivalence" and "positive discrimination". In the post-Communist CEE, among other regions, othering as well as "identity project" manifest a fundamental angle of study of identity groups in post-colonial States. Generally, it is based on those majority and minority relations that are drawn around boundaries imposed upon both societal categories and built up with the attempt to protect one's identity from another, in order to protect both at the same time. For example, this positive discrimination has been so far used in CEE for the description of the role of ethno-linguistic minorities of Russian people in the Baltic States, such as in Latvia (Cheskin 2016), as well as in the case of the post-Yugoslavian Croatia's discourse on national selfhood with respect to ethnic minorities.

Regarding these two interesting examples of positive discrimination, Latvia's Russian speakers are all considered "equally different" to others regardless of their social, cultural, educational, and political differences. Unlike other phenomena of potential change throughout the Soviet era, a clear process of othering did not only come to consolidate political and cultural hegemonic majoritarian model in post-Soviet Latvia. Such othering does continue, perhaps subtly, or inconspicuously, to construct a more negative perception of separateness between Latvian-ness and Russian speakers, the majority of whom are Latvians. Also in the post-Yugoslavian Croatia, similar to Kundera's geo-cultural division of Europe in search of that Western-ness faded away due to the Soviet takeover and further standardised policy in Central Europe, the country attempted to distance itself from the stereotypical stigma of "orientalism" and "backwardness" that in the 1990s the Balkan Peninsula began to be associated with. Interestingly enough, such othering occurred as a radical otherness also for Slovenia after the dissolution of the previous regime[3]. This has offered intriguing perspectives for the study of national selfhood and foreign policy strategies based on an understanding of the Balkan identity as something "other" for the newly-established Slovenian and Croatian power institutions. It seems paradoxical how the reference to "Balkan identity" has become in recent years the least desirable option for the future of both countries.

Besides essentialist and circumstantialist literature, of particular interest is yet another approach that came to theoretically criticise both approaches over identity issues. With regards to repeatedly reinforcing reflection of a "Self" and an "Other", a combination of critical theory over cultural as well as psychoanalytic aspects of identity building has pointed out that "identity problems" cannot be reduced to a binary approach of "fixed identity" (e.g., pre-given at birth and a-historically) against "multiple identities" (e.g., contingent factors related to time and space) and vice versa. This angle of investigation along with its categories of understanding identity deals dialogically, therefore dialectically, with all relations that occur in between the "Self" and the

---

[3] Nataša, Zambelli, in "Evolving Identities: A Poststructuralist Analysis of Croatia's Approach to Minority Rights," at the UACES 38th Annual Conference, Edinburgh, 1–3 September 2008.

"Other" (Taylor 1992: 34). In the attempt to unravel a large number of several layers of national, sub-national, supranational, and overlapping forms of group identities, which may also coexist from within at the same time, this scholarship is linked to the responsible person's voluntary choice to try to give the most appropriate form to their life (Viola 2008: 525). As Makariev noted, this contemporary philosophical approach towards community identity is particularly popular among philosophers and critical thinkers coming from a postmodern background (2017) or, also well-known, from the poststructuralist scholarship. In general, they mostly tend to look beneath the apparently simple spatial (here) and temporal (now) subjectivity of identities. In this vein, the approach of poststructuralist theory began to offer a review of normative concepts to which minority groups may be ascribed for a social order (e.g., power structure) they are positioned in. By doing so, they have left room for a newly-fresh approach over minority issues, which is not only used over the linguistic investigation but also encompasses other aspects of minority identities. In this regard, unlike both scholarships of essentialism and structuralism, identity is understood as a polymorphous and unstable entity that tends to change over time.

Overall, the scholarly tendency to conflate poststructuralism and postmodernism comes from the result of Habermas's idea on poststructuralist claims that could be viewed as those of "Young Conservatives" (Spivak 1999: 312). Nonetheless, poststructuralism has gained popularity in academic circles as it refers to a range of theoretical notions developed in the second half of the twentieth century from which philosophical movements have come to challenge the general rules and modernist notions of the philosophy of language (Sausserean structuralism) and Strauss phenomenology (Karim and Anjum 2016: 36). This philosophical movement is often associated with Jacques Derrida and his work of examination of the notion of difference in all its facets as well as a radical questioning of otherness and subject-object relation (Lechte 2018: 128). Derrida, among others, has recently offered interesting lenses to deepen the understanding of the world from a different perspective since he has built a decentred island of language and culture with philosophical logic.

However, similar to essentialism and structuralism, poststructuralism lacks a coherent and uniform notion for defining its methodological approach(es). Without any doubt, it contributes to giving yet another, perhaps more satisfactory, panoptic perspective through which the tandem identity and culture could be properly investigated and better grasped. It has generally shifted the discussion from the terrain where essentialism and constructivism stand in opposition, toward the opportunity to focus all identity-related concerns through both unifying and divisive forces that the same notion of identity owns in-itself. In particular, poststructuralism has not only referred to socio-political identities through multi-layered existing facets, but it does mainly focus on the crucial role of new aspects of social subjects (Laclau and Mouffe 1985) whereby essentialism and structuralism are no longer capable of theoretically sustaining the practical fluidity of a given group's identity within or across certain boundaries.

To a certain extent, poststructuralists give credit to the intricate, albeit inconspicuous, constellation of interconnectedness between Selves and Others rather than trying through bizarre attempts to compromise different identities along equipollent lines. In this, poststructuralism contributes to seeing categories of "difference" as close to a structure while remaining utterly heterogeneous vis-à-vis the structure itself (Laclau 2000: 76). Poststructuralists thus view identity as a non-unitary trait that changes over time (Smith 2016) and depict the subject as diverse, contradictory, dynamic, and changing over historical time and social space (Norton 2000: 125). Under certain circumstances, this approach focusses on the several "selves" that a subject—either individually or collectively—may possess and how a certain situation can activate them. In the process of self-identification, for example, the latter can never end up in an "achieved identity" which might be presupposed by specific ethno-national group interests (Fearon 1988, Hardin 1995), in case of a minority identity. In keeping this perspective, what here could be interpreted as a seemingly chaotic perception of the poststructuralist view of identity can be better understood in a specific and narrowed-down context. As an example, Judith Butler in her *Gender Trouble* identifies poststructuralism as the rejection of the claims that totality and universality (2000: 36) in open critique towards some theorists, such as David Laitin among others, whose interpretation of personal identities follows a largely essentialist interpretation that rests primarily on genetics and specific histories (1998: 16).

Nowadays, the question of each identity's multiple selves seems to have become an object of controversy within recent philosophical scholarship and cultural debate in the wider public. However, the so-called "Inner Self" possessing many deep layers that can be exposed only through private introspection, goes back to Martin Luther's philosophical contribution. As Fukuyama noted, Luther is metaphorically responsible for such understanding of multiple Selves. However, while Luther's "Inner Self" did not seek out recognition for its potential newfound freedom or form of being (2018:28), nowadays it has become openly public and political. As a matter of fact, LGBTQI+ communities, among others, have recently increased their campaigns for public recognition and socially accepted coexistence of sexual identities within yet other identities (e.g., ethnicity, religion, nationality, political membership, and so forth) which they may also be, or not be, directly correlated with.

Interestingly enough, poststructuralist scholarship may also be dated back to Jean-Jacques Rousseau's affirmation of inner identities depending on, and asserted by, the so-called "perfectionability" of being. Besides being fundamentally good, Rousseau's perfectionability is a source of limitless potential which may be unfolded in the attempt to satisfy human desire for happiness and liberation of the Self from the artificial constraints of society (mentioned by Fukuyama 2018: 98). In *Being Transgender and Transgender Being*, Sophie Grice Chappell recalls a new approach over gender identity within feminism, gender studies, and queer theories. Building a thought-provoking argumentation upon what Stuart Mill in his *On Liberty* (1859) calls "experiments in living", Chappell buys a kind of essentialist feminism by reaffirming the widespread idea that "sex is nature, gender is nurture" (2018: 27). The latter implies that natural sex is not a matter of choice unless it is not subjected to transitioning process, while, conversely, gender representation is a matter of choice that reinforces the idea of the politicality of the sex (Žižek 2017: 198). In this case, and not only, poststructuralism cannot be understood as a coherent movement (Karim and Anjum 2016). To a certain extent, it is also quite hard to coherently differentiate philosophical nuances of both approaches of structuralism and poststructuralism. What makes these two philosophical scholarships different is that structuralism (i.e., circumstantialism) investigates facts of human life through their interrelations which constitute structures. Conversely, poststructuralism disputes this approach. In fact, the latter presents different critiques of structuralism as a dismissal of the self-sufficiency of the structures. At the same time, poststructuralism questions the binary opposition that confronts structures with human agencies, and vice versa, thereby centralising these two poles of confrontation and presenting them as fixed, static, finalised, and lastly authoritative.

As some scholars have critically affirmed (Spivak 1999, Karim 2016, and others), poststructuralism does not have anything new to offer. However, as Schwandner-Sievers pointed out, structuralist approaches tend to risk essentialising cultures and societies due to their emphasis on the supposed static dichotomy between "structure" and "agency", thereby shaping people's attitudes and behaviour (2019: 22). In other words, while all potential postmodern theories seem to be a kind of repetition, they hand on the presence of a subject (agency) in a postmodern hyperspace (structure) where the latter may feel the loss of identity. Poststructuralism could best address the trajectory of issues-within-an-issue in the much-discussed field of "cultural identities". For instance, it could better navigate through a large variety of internal, multiple, multi-layered, often intersectional, sometimes hidden or consciously buried forms of identities. Despite the fact that poststructuralism complicates models of investigation by radicalising some structuralist premises (Finkelde 2013), the latter cannot undermine the method through which poststructuralists look at both issues of identity and culture. Depicting an identity as a diverse, contradictory, and dynamic being in constantly change over time within social spaces (Norton, 2000: 125) means to understand identity as a relational term which defines the relationship between two or more related entities in a manner that asserts a difference, similarity, or equality. In this sense, poststructuralism is a rupture with the previous philosophical approaches.

Similar to individual identities, hence poststructuralists sustain that modes of creation of a group identity—of a communitarian "We"—cannot be considered as internally monolithic. Even in those cases where members align themselves with the same community they are members of, they do overlook internal, perhaps hidden, often repressed, modes of thinking, different ways of living, socio-economic backgrounds, and other infinite differences which are impossible to deny. In these cases, poststructuralism sheds light on the Self and a construction that happens not only due to a process of othering, but also due to not-yet-recognised selves that have different degrees of otherness and that may play a crucial role for further transformation. Within the sphere of so-called Minority Studies, such poststructuralist approach has come to define the issues of non-recognised "minorities-within-a-minority", such as the presence of LGBTQI+ communities within the Muslim minority, or Shia-Sunni division within Islamic tradition, and so forth. For instance, also Derrida pointed out in his conversation with the Algerian intellectual Chérif Mustafa (2008) that there are many Islams just as there are many Wests. In that event, Derrida insisted that living together requires a recognition of the interruption of identity and presence to self that occurs within each of us and in our relations to each other. In addressing each other, indeed, the Muslim and the Westerner are given as overstating their identities as Muslim and Westerner, respectively. Each is given as possessing a singular idiom, a singular way of being, which is untranslatable into the general idioms of the substantial ensembles. The principle of civilisation, Derrida argues, lies in the respect for the alterity of the singular idioms (2004).

It is here clear that an understanding of the degree of otherness within the Self does not concern only the Self, but also the "Other's other". It is a process of mutual contamination that operates from both directions at the same time. This moves away from constructivism, for example, whose approach of both positively and negatively constructed identity follows the radical differences between the Self and the Other. It also unpacks the same processes of identity construction without undermining differences in sociopolitical context or dismissing the moment-to-moment construct of identity (Smith 2016:256). It interestingly opens the door to another strategy to have a look beneath, and not at, a given group identity. It gives the idea of a matter that has become subtler and more complex in general. In few words, the poststructuralist view of identity does not only deny essentialist claims over uniqueness of the existence of a being, but it also deals differently with the contingent products of categorisation of people along a binary of the Self and the Other and their further constructed activities of being. It simply tackles identity issues as phenomena in a state in flux (Smith 2016:255).

The "Self" and the "Other" are only two sites of a struggle, which begins to take place from within at first, and whose extensions have overlapped each other in the past few years. As Smith manages to clarify, this "site of struggle" does not place the Self and the Other in rigid opposition one against another. However, it calls for a given interaction between one's self that is portraying to the people it is interacting with, and when the latter grasps and achieves the notion of the self that it wants to acquire, a negotiation has already overtaken and bridged them (2016:255). This reference of identity seen through "a site of struggle" and being constantly established and revised within an interaction between the Self and the Other, is a useful strategy to settle a deeper investigation over minority issues.

In between the so far highly overused, contrasting dichotomy of essentialism and constructivism, poststructuralism tackles the lack of common definition of culture and identity by denying any kind of invariable specificity of the existence of a pure being. The latter can be easily deconstructed and reconstructed around different spatio-temporal nodal points and constantly reinterpreted with the use of different parameters. In other words, such process is ongoing and never reaches an end-point. Although almost identical to structuralism in considering identity as a form of (minority) becoming, and focussing on the "process"

(Block 2007) of an unstated being, which is contextually driven and that it might emerge from interactions thanks to a given discourse (Miyaharay 2010). However, it gives a philosophical framework for analysing contemporary age of vernacular politics, surmounting the limitations of new social sciences and strands of multiculturalism as well as cosmopolitanism. Hence, seeing identity as a state in flux refers to the above-mentioned idea of becoming and unbecoming, which happens in a space that is nowadays a reference of better representing, deeper understanding, and oftentimes even resisting both the world and the culture of the people existing in it. It follows that poststructuralists view "identity" as a non-unitary trait that changes over time (Smith 2016:254). This seemingly chaotic perception, however, which includes both contradictory attempts to differentiate and integrate a sense of self along with different social dimensions (e.g., gender, race, socio-economic status, ethnicity, class, nation, regional territory), it is nevertheless a mode of inquiry that emphasises both interferences and intermingling between majoritarian cultural system and minority groups.

At the forefront of the poststructuralism scholarship, Jacques Derrida's theory of deconstruction is understood in terms of a philosophical act for radically criticising the traditional approach of structuralism. In general, poststructuralist strategies refer oftentimes to gender studies and their society-related issues in the public wider, such as what it means to be fully recognised as a man rather than a woman, as a gay man instead of a lesbian, and so forth. In general, Derrida's deconstruction is one of the most interesting manoeuvres to secure postmodernism as a philosophical movement that aims to correctly problematize assumed ideas related to the construction of a specific individual identity, destroying internalisation of categories and structural necessity for an identity to be. It therefore unravels strategies of stigmatization and culturally internalised stigmas to those they are ascribed to. In particular, Derrida's philosophical purpose of deconstructing may aim to counterweight externally imposed construction of identity, particularly "malignant" identity buildings from within the Self. Although his "de-constructivism" deals mainly with the sphere of language and discursive identity strategies, it is yet another useful method of reading the construction of politicality among minority groups. In this regard, whether any collective Self cannot be separated from constantly engaged actions of (re-)constituting in relation to the world through sense of alternative identification (Mouffe 2000:148), deconstruction is here a merely guided process of identification that digs into nodal points around which an identity is formed. Thus, whether process of identification can never lead to a kind of "already achieved" identity status, deconstructing means nothing other than disentangling all categorisation of identity (e.g., "Armenian" rather than "Turkish", "white" rather than "indigenous", "working class" rather than "intellectual") ascribed to a subject at various time and space (e.g., speeches, policy statements, media interview, and so forth).

If one could speculate over yet another frontman of the poststructuralist approach, Jacques Lacan, while for structuralism approach identity is a matter of mirroring itself, for poststructuralists identity has to look at itself in a series of distorting mirrors (Soldado 2019:10).

Some, especially among essentialists, might here argue and point out that such deconstruction could be the veiled destructive attempt to bury all aspects of a given culture or identity in nullity. Conversely, it is here that poststructuralism leaves behind the redundant way of defining the term "cultural identity". After all, what is produced from a critical thinking reflects philosophical willingness to (re-)examine contested and highly controversial aspects making the realm not liveable. In addition, deconstructing does not mean, or aim to, nullify identities and render them cultureless. It instead concerns the contemporary way of understanding how identity constructions occur without wishing to bury aspects of a specific culture or identity around which the same construction has been built up, somewhat imposed. In this perspective, deconstructing is a shot at unshackling critical thinking from institutionalised philosophy which questions in a radical way the supremacy of any concept such as that of "identity" (Karim and Anjum 2016:39). In this case, an act of deconstructing gains a positive intent since it aims at opposing one's culture claim by insider and outsiders as well as the notion of culture as a nice name for the exoticism of the global, national, or local outsiders. Deconstructing aims thus to disentangle externally imposed as well as internally constructed malignant history of ontology of a being—namely, of a subject, which goes along with its cultural facets that in turn belong essentially from the formulation of the question of the same being, whose real investigation is possible solely within its formulation[4]. Similar to the postcolonial studies, with regard to minority groups, too, this deconstructing serves positively for decreasing political polarizations, cultural frictions, and hegemonic ambitions of the most powerful groups with regard to particular social orders they rule culturally over. In other words, deconstructing

---

[4] Allusion to the so-called Derridean (theory of) deconstruction. See more Christopher Kul-Want & Piero. *Introducing Continental Philosophy – a Graphic Guide*, London:Omnibus Business Centre, 2013:123-124.

challenges systems-based diametrical opposites called binary oppositions (i.e., Self and Others = majoritarian cultural system and minority groups), hierarchies (i.e., those who govern and those who are governed) and paradoxes (i.e., unrecognised groups from within a recognised collective Self and Otherness) in all the fields of life. To put it simply, deconstructing is philosophically aimed at breaking power structures and hegemonies of social order, focussing on the idiosyncrasies of an identity in order to create tolerance and forbearance on the one hand, and bring any stereotypes to an end, on the other one. In the very end, a deconstruction project aims at refusing the construction of a us-versus-them paradigm, which is deeply rooted in promoting an in-group loyalty and out-group hostility.

Firstly because it is constantly interrogating the dialogical binary of the "Self" towards the "Other", and vice versa, shedding light on how majoritarian cultural systems posit "otherness". In so doing, the poststructuralist approach unpacks such Self-and-Other relation by opening up a perspective from which practices and discourses show what kind of nodal points and parameters are used to construct otherness. From a minority perspective, this aims to shed light on those members of minority groups who need to develop their skills in the wider public, such as how to exercise their free speech rights. Moreover, considering any type of identity as a result of construction within a specific realm and power structures, it does not necessarily mean that just because a specific group of people is constructed in a particular way by another, the group actually shares views and behavioural patterns ascribed to it. As Ilisei refers to in the Romanian cases, some minority groups do not even recognise themselves as such (2017:62). More than using a structure within which a construction of an identity is possible, post-constructivism affirms how Self-and-Other relations are never an outcome of a unidirectional process of construction but involved instead into a dialectical movement from above (e.g. top-down) and from below (e.g. bottom-up) at the same time.

At this point, several implications can be made over the notion of minority through the point of view of poststructuralism and its followers. Against, for example, the usage of the socio-politically accepted nomenclature, definitions, categorisations, and explorations of social realms that through divisive paradigms construct groups and their identities to be "majority" and "minority". Rather than highlighting the "real" issues between dominant positions versus subordinate ones that old-fashioned ways to describe groups along religious, ethnic, or racial affiliations tend to overlook, I label as extremely porous the category of majority and minority. Both are visibly undergoing substantial variations since they have ceased to regulate group cling to symbol of ethnicity and religion, but they have been externally and vertically imposed through hegemonic power structures of states or emperors.

In other words, decades onwards from the time when the notion of, and the legal term for, "minority" gained visibility and relevancy worldwide, the same minority boundaries around which the definition was constructed have become porous. While the relation with "a non-dominant position whose members [...] possess ethnic, religious or linguistics characteristics differing from those of the rest of the population" shows an ambiguous way for the centrality of such numerical factor (Makariev 2017), the growth of hidden, yet not fully recognised, issues within "a minority" shed light on the multiple identities that an extremely instrumentalist-constructivist approach had overlooked in the aftermaths of the Second World War. Due to the multiplicity within each socio-political identity, which presents intersectional facets overlapping among its selves and with those of the "other", the notion of "minority" has begun to question parallel ethnic, racial, gender parameters by which different people have been so far classified and attributed to (Ali 2004). In turn, it poses an intriguing question with regard to whether or not the categorisation of majority and minority as a societal leaves space for those minorities within a minority excluded because they are not yet recognised.

For example, among others, use of new categorisation of minorities, such as RAE (minority composed of people with Roma, Askhali, Egyptian origins) within the Roma people, have appeared along with new attention paid to those case studies where no real difference between minority and majoritarian cultural systems has been drawn. A few publications focussing on the Aromanian minorities across the Balkan region have voiced the opinion that today none belonging to that transnational community seems to maintain, and gets advantages from, their recognised minority status in comparison with the larger society (Kahl, 2002:169). Paradoxically, indeed, even though minority status is recognised and minority rights guaranteed, the majority of Balkan Aromanians behave like the members of the majoritarian cultural systems of the Nations they live in, with the only exception language affiliation (2002:149). A deadlock of classification is clearly discernible through the constant attempt to identify Hungary's Roma minority and the search for a correct definition for LGBTQI+ communities. In the first case, members of Hungary's Roma communities have a dual identity. They consider themselves as belonging both to the Hungarian people and to the smaller Roma families. This is why the so called "Roma question" has historically remained central on Hungary's political and cultural agenda (Bársony and Daróczi 2018:7). In the second case, instead, Žižek touches upon the use of the symbol "+". The latter, which is supposed to identify all subjectivities, opens the door to a potential inclusion of all stand-in sexual orientations and thereby gives "a body" to the formula LGBTQI+ (2017:208). Last but not least, from an epistemological perspective, the recent rise of populism has misled the minority-majority binary, misleading the same concept of being potentially exposed to diverse threats or violations. Many populist governments in CEE, indeed, have oftentimes presented themselves as resisting political actors to the hegemonic discourse of liberalism (see conclusion) in the name of diversity and even minority rights, as if to say, "We Hungarians" or, "We Poles", and so forth, represent nowadays the minorities within the European Union, whose set of traditional values and moral norms represent the "one-size-must-fit-all" universalism promoted by Western elitism (Müller 2017:56).

From the perspective of multiculturalism, despite the fact that most of the definitions and categories of "majority" and "minority" go along lines of "majoritarian culturally dominant system" versus "subaltern and dominated minority group", the latter and the former are neither qualitative nor quantitative characteristics. They only refer to the relative position of the parties involved in relations of economic, political, and institutional power (Patton 2010:68), which have recently become insignificant. This dichotomy is thus a self-made politics creation aimed at referring to, and being used as, an operational category of institutionalized prescriptive practices into scientific disciplines, especially among social sciences, rather than one of deep analysis. It is clearly revealed, and useful, in the lexical analysis of media coverage, social research, or other legal and official documents in general, that they have become an academic habit and accepted way to continue to certify and produce the already-sedimented layers of canonical knowledge (Marchart 2018:161). The dichotomy itself, as Kołodziejczyk noted, can be easily criticised because it extremely simplifies a complicated relation of the Self's and Other's selves into a flat binarism of collective I/the "Other" (2010:129). From a minority perspective, the same category of "minority" in reflection to the one of the majoritarian cultural system, has in time imposed a symbolic type of inequality and existence of inequality. By default, such use of the majority and minority paradigm, which externally imposes an ascription to minorities through the category of "subaltern" as well as "unequal" and "different", continues to perpetuate a nonlinear ground in terms of a different degree of, or even complete lack of, civil, political, and economic differences. Such "one-dimensional endeavour projects a taken-for-granted image of unbridgeable condition which does not reflect an interrogation of the Self and the Other, and vice versa. It seems that both Self and Other do not possess only one distinctive being from within. On the contrary, they both tend to repress others from within, while being in their struggle of recognition and putting them not only into a vis-à-vis confrontation, but also into an internal confrontation with layers of themselves.

CHAPTER THREE

Post-Communism and Post-Colonialism: Do They Mirror Each Other?

In the constant attempt to explore new intersectional aspects in the post-Communist societies, application of the post-colonial perspective in CEE gained popularity among scholars and practitioners. Whether or not a post-colonial CEE exists, seems to have become one of the most fascinating questions to raise and investigate.

Following Frantz Fanon's sociopolitical analysis in his *The Wretched of the Earth* (1961), the legacy of the post-colonial period is found deeply rooted in nations across the Global South (e.g., Latin America, Africa, Southeast Asia). By being largely influenced by the Continental tradition of philosophy, such as Michel Foucault's discursive analysis and Jacques Derrida's concept of deconstruction (Braeunlien 2014: 3) among others, the post-colonial paradigm has been barely transferred in the post-Communist academia in CEE. Although a wide range of theoretical experiments, research, and projection of post-colonialism in the former Eastern Bloc compose an abundant field of reference, its approach has so far failed to gain large interest, perhaps for the too provocative Marxist sympathies that the owners of such scholarship have and stand for. Above all, the field of Post-Colonial Studies as well as poststructuralism (or post-modernism) have utterly failed to cohabit with the strong anti-Communist sentiment that civil societies stemmed from and later developed throughout the post-1989 transformation and transition toward full-fledged democracies.

As time passed by the fall of the Berlin Wall, pluralism and multiculturalism in the region have been exclusively presented as a theoretical framework and space of further concord and harmony. Yet, both have utterly failed under the parapet of an externally imposed discourse of post-Communist dystopian mood or, interestingly enough, of nostalgic as well as utopic contributions for an entirely new society to come. It followed that minority issues had been largely and intensively investigated through the lens of the dual debate of liberalism versus communitarianism (e.g., Taylor 1979, MacIntyre 1981, Sandel 1982, Walzer 1983, Kymlicka 1989, Avineri and De-Shalit 1992); between the interwoven relationships of recognition and distribution (Fraser 1995, 2000; Tully 2000; Fraser and Honneth 2003); the so called "essential versus construct" dilemma as well as the danger of essentialism and the role of hybridity (Young 1990, 2000; Benhabib 1995, 1996a; Butler 1990; Appiah 2004, Makariev 2017); the limits of tolerance, or the relationship between the collective minority rights and individual citizenship rights (Kymlicka 1995b; Spinner 1994, 2000); and State protection of territorial integrity and maintenance of national security with regard to certain implementation of self-governing platforms, federalism, or parallel power structures (Bebgy and Burges 2009).

These interdisciplinary attempts aimed at merging poles of confrontation (e.g., liberal multiculturalism, the theory of tolerance towards illiberal groups, cosmopolitan approach over local affairs) have been in turn discarded due to the critical viewpoints that stress out theoretical idiosyncrasies and practical paradoxes. Despite the importance of these dimensions, it would be possible to affirm that they do not compose an exhaustive list of themes if applied over the post-Communist European region. Within this array of approaches, the post-colonial perspective is scholarly useful to represent an alternative angle of investigation which is aimed at stressing out how power action of dispossessing, discarding and setting aside "Other's knowledge" occurs through a subtler and lasting power-organised cultural operation of patronisation. In regard to the purpose of this study, such perspective cannot exclusively explore how Western-led projects of democratisation have been historically folded into a Eurocentric form of ventriloquism where Eurocentric values, under The Universal Declaration of Human Rights, and in the very end, prefer to (secretly) speak on behalf of the Western promoters rather than for the local needy. These are, indeed, as Žižek correctly argues, the two sides of the same ideological mystification: the imposition of Western values, on the one side, and respect for different cultures independently of the horrors that can be part of these cultures (2017: 198), on the other side.

Because all of these, the post-colonial perspective is simply a scholarly attempt to shed a new light on how post-socialist trajectory of power that CEE nations began to experience since 1989 while masking strife for shaping a realm of coexistence by colonially imposing an identity-manoeuvring and behaviour-forming process upon certain segments of peoples (Bársony and Daróczi 2018: 4). In their attempts to achieve coherence, it seemed that post-Communist countries adapted smarter nation-building policies that would have reified the imagines of their suppressed national identities free to be effectively constructed with symbols and histories that national identities were stolen from

(Castellino 2018: 344). In the meantime, such process took place along with the rise of a new set of new rules of the political game, in which formerly Soviet instrument of power and domination were turned into new ones. Typical for post-colonial countries, the reversion of power structures brought those who most benefit from the backdrop of Communism, to act according to what seemed for them to be justified (Chomsky 1999: 9) after the cruelty and injustice they have suffered. However, in the very end, they began also to hide their vested interests thanks to the rise of new forms of moralistic righteousness.

In the meantime, the interwoven issues of identity and diversity have engulfed the post-Communist region of Europe in the post-1989 era. It particularly continues nowadays to leave room to scholars to label the region, especially in its peripheries, such as the Balkan Penisula and the entire Caucasus, as a semi-peripheral region where the coexistence with "the Other" is getting even more difficult that it was in the past. From a (post-)colonial point of view, a certain picture of the "Oriental" over the region projects the region itself behind a space that is not Europe anymore but shadowed by the reflection of the Orient, that is, a place uncontaminated by modernisation which stems from a more cultural than the geographical dichotomy between "Occident-and-Orient". In this way, religious and ethnic divisions across the region are often put at the use of people in power for concealing deeper contradictions in their societies (Spickard 2010: 131).

Given this token, both post-Communism and post-colonialism have been followed, and continue to be, by vacuumed political programs of inclusion. Rather than contriving intervals between which divisions and separations continue to remain at the disposal of political interpretations and their further objectives, old-fashioned approaches are solely interested to set up tables of intriguing discussions and disputes. Once again, rather than establishing a space to fairly conduct interaction between academia and policy implementation, they continue to remain powerless in light of the large number of issues at stake.

On the one hand, it would seem that post-colonialism and its scholars (e.g. Gayatri Chakravorty Spivak, Edward Said, and Homi K. Bhabha) have little to offer in comparison with the 1980s structuralist scholarship. On the other hand, it would also seem theoretically risky to simply apply post-colonial paradigms across the post-socialist space in the attempt to include newly arrived cultural perspectives and challenges (Tlostanova 2012: 332).

Madina Tlostanova refuses a complete application of the post-colonial paradigm over the successor republics of the Soviet Union and its formerly satellite region. In this regard, she does not consider "Soviet colonialisation" as such indeed; rather, she considers the latter as a "second class empire" rather than a "first class" similar to those that resulted from Western colonial experiences, such as those of Great Britain, France, Spain, and Portugal. Similarly, Dorota Kołodzieijczuk pointed critically out that a post-colonial paradigm in the post-Communist CEE brings more problems than benefits since its "owners", together with their academic institutions involved in poststructuralist discourse, are for many reasons incorrect. (2010: 125–140). Or, perhaps, she specified that a post-colonial investigation missed the chance to include CEE (minority) resistance during the '80s and '90s. Since then, both case and concept of "Soviet imperialism" were not enough developed and taken into account (2010: 133–134). In fact, the "Soviets" were not understood as "colonisers" in toto, despite the fact that in post-colonial discourse even the earlier Nazi idea for the whole of Europe was a typical projection of a potential (and veritable) colony (Fanon 2011: 80). Perhaps, the lingering problems of racism and ideological prison-style Nation's "Proletarian superiority" over all classes were not blatantly colonial in their forms of existence. Veiled by the party-state rhetoric and dictatorship, which trumpeted the virtues of egalitarianism and internationalism, the "Soviets" were not "too colonial". However, there are points of convergences. As Van Harpen argued, the Communist demise from European lands has never been explained through the fallacy of the Russian identity's messianism at work through a process of expansionism which ceased to preserve its colonial order and imperial fatigue. Such Russian identity was indeed preserved during the Communist experience and nurtured by an orthodox religious outlook that turned the proclamation of the dictatorship of the Proletariat into an autocracy, the Marxism-Leninism into a new form of orthodoxy, the historical community (Общность) of the Soviet People forced into the only one constitutive ruling ethnos (Kushnir 2018: 62, 25), namely, the Russian one.

To a certain extent, it would be also possible to agree on such critical viewpoint against post-colonial theory. Or, if not entirely colonised, the region of the former Eastern Bloc could be understood as a historically semicolonial region, such as Thailand (Jackson 2010, mentioned by Braeunlein 2014), where the relation to the power is as ambiguous as the relation with the other, the foreigner, the alien (Braeunlein 2014). Given this token it is possible to trace how that "giving a say" to voiceless discourse began to unleash and thereby strengthen a significantly deconstructive impetus of national voices trapped within the prison-style ideological orbit of Communism. It followed that national minority nations were brought into a new emerging path that would have seemed to align Kundera's recall for essentialism against Communist dominancy. Similarly, Dariusz Skorczewaki referred to both Russian and Western cultures as a discursively hegemonic reflection upon Europe in general, and Poland in particular, in the process of embodying stereotypes of inferiority through ascription of otherness. Without any doubt, the aftermath of the Communist demise was a clear manifestation of a wide range of one's own subjectivity (e.g., collective, national, political) previously negated by an imperial discourse and accompanied by a simultaneous criticism of the collective national subject in favour of the homo sovieticus or the Great Proletariat. It was even clearer how such deconstruction of the collective subject came to mobilise voiceless national minorities that emerged from circumstances they were subject to. As a result, extremely similar to post-colonial states (Castellino 2018: 344), post-Communist successor states emerged with a mass of communities, including some that were historically antagonistic or highly confrontational toward each other, and others nurturing new forms of antagonism construed, constructed, and even nourished by a long-term period of colonial "divide and rule" policies. A wide range of phenomena of exclusion that were at work in the post-1989 era.

The paradoxical facet of such "minority affirmation" is not given by a deconstructive management model of the previous collective subjectivities that embodied successfully an insurrection project. Of course, the latter remains a fundamental aspect, yet differently understood from the mainstream projection of political antagonism or confrontation. However, it is for the basis on which de-colonisation of the former Eastern Bloc came to take action by excluding and setting apart those who were already excluded in the previously constructed political and cultural realm of domination. For example, it is interesting to interrogate the euphoria of the "return to Europe" that post-Communist countries experienced, and how the latter began to exclude certain groups of population from Europe itself. Among others, for example, the presence of autochthonous Muslim groups living on the Balkans, more precisely, inhabiting their lands of origin, has not yet managed to include their socio-cultural role in the vision of Europe (Shenk 2006: 20). This perspective opens yet another dilemma through which it is comprehensible how a certain fabrication of colonial superiority-and-inferiority remains as such in space and time. Typically instructive is here the example of the Serbia-oriented Yugoslavian policy toward Kosovo, which was somehow understood as a Serbian colony. The latter came indeed to be associated with the dominant ideology ignited by historical events and aggressive infiltration of Serbian politics into all sphere of life (Naumonić 2002: 16), where a kind of Serbian hegemonic force of the former Yugoslavia toward other Socialist Republics' populations did not cease to exist due to a quasi-colonizing attitude of the Belgrade-centralised power. In fact, although Yugoslavia was doomed years before 1991, prior to the definitive collapse, reduction of other "republics" to "provinces" was part of the Serb nationalist policy. From a Kosovo perspective, one might even surpass standards of slander with the openly racist characterisation of Kosovo people and the region itself, which in Serbia continues to be understood as a country with no formal economy and run, in effect, by criminal gangs that traffic in drugs, contraband and women. This is centrally paramount to understand one of the most problematic paradoxes that the Western wider public could not really grasp during the Yugoslavia dissolution wars in the 1990s. For instance, when Western media covered the grassroots opposition to Slobodan Milosevic's Socialist Party's falsification of 1996 elections passionately, but they overlooked what demonstrators were screaming during the anti-Milosevic protests: "Instead of kicking us out, go to Kosovo and kick Albanians out!" (Žižek 2017: 229,126). Against such pitfall, in today's Serbia the absolute *sine qua non* of an authentic political act would be to reject the ideological, and thus political, topos of the Albanian threat in Kosovo (Žižek 2000: 126).

Therefore, what is today equally recognised as an aggressive form of nationalism with tendencies toward paranoia or collective hysteria, fuelled by banal forms of national identities under the name of "popular will" which seems to form a long-term "organic crisis" (See Part Two) that post-Communist apparatus has left in CEE. From "a minority perspective", some would identify such "organic crisis" as a factual post-colonial phenomenon (Terian 2012: 23). Both externally imposed ascription of exotic downgrading other's culture and assertion of forms of cultural backwardness, poses a sharper correlation between the post-Communist and the post-colonial conceptualisation with regard to identifying issues such as hybridity, in-betweenness, and liminality of those who have been left behind. In fact, it would not appear so heretic to juxtapose the paradigm of the post-colonial with post-Communist. If the typically identifiable post-colonial states across the globe adopted majoritarian identities as "national" identities, dismissing the "Other's" into another (subaltern) position to be accommodated, moderated, challenged, or even eliminated because seen and understood as a potential threat (Castellino 2018: 345–346), the same phenomenon happened to the post-Communist states in CEE. Without dismissing critical viewpoints and scepticism over the correlation of the two posts, the (post-)colonial paradigm cannot be understood as a new theory of humanism aimed at empowering marginalised or excluded communities. If critically applied upon performing acts as well as acts to be performed by excluded and omitted subcultures in a colonised realm, such paradigm digs simply into how a certain imposition of inferiority is externally ascribed upon a certain group. Beyond any doubt, the patterns of post-Communism have been at the centre of academic debate due to the rise of newly-fresh, albeit valid, interdisciplinary fields of research (e.g., "Sovietology", "Soviet Studies", "Balkanology", "Balkan Studies", and so forth). In this, the post-colonial paradigm is neither seen as an "identity manifesto" as someone could easily claim, nor as a slightly more theoretically redefined "identity policy programme", which would seem to have already shown a repetitive project of cultural ethnicisation in its outputs. It is instead a process for shedding light on imposed discursive hegemonic ascription upon those deprived to speak as an independently recognised subject—no matter if collective or individual one. Although the decision to use post-colonialism in post-Communist societies is a risky path to take, the latter may lead towards a critical analytical instrument to unravel identity issues by digging up mechanisms of subordination that certain groups are subject to, navigating, thus revealing, those nodal points and structures around and between which cultural backwardness and political subaltern status are imposed on.

More generally, post-colonial theory sets the scene for a reflection throughout the pre- and post-emerging (hegemonic) conditions, which are seen in a continuum, along which a given group in the form of minority came to appear as a *qua* minority and forced instrumentally into a subaltern position. In this regard, this category of "post" is not (or not exclusively) a mere description of "after the end of" a certain historical epoch. In addition, it is a deeper look at what happened "after the beginning of" a certain historical epoch without following necessarily the chronology-centred methodology of history based on a recollection of facts and events. In particular, indeed, the post-colonial paradigm enables us to dig into the between-ness created within a space of a "not-yet-concluded" epoch. The latter was understood by Antonio Gramsci who referred to such continuum in terms of "organic crisis", namely, a period in which the old is dying but the new cannot be born (op. cit. 1971). Within this, a hegemonic discourse and behaviour patterns are about to be imposed for shaping a new direction in social life from within an interregnum where a certain knowledge is about to emerge thanks to an ideological apparatus which continues to face the insidious remnant of the previously established discourse (Terian 2012: 22). Hence, the post-colonial fabrication of subalternity onto "the Other" mirrors the post-communist one's, where a similar power fabrication continues to impose ambivalence onto certain segments of the society which penetrates and affects the realm of the everyday life (Lomba 1998). To a certain extent, one might pinpoint that a status of subalternity is paradoxically internalised, and oftentimes (un)consciously accepted in order to seek benefits out of it. From this point of view, while in CEE many claim that minority groups suffer from an "incomplete becoming" due to a lack of cultural prior to a political recognition in the wider public (Fukuyama 2018, Taylor 1992), minority groups do not only suffer from their incapability to deconstruct a collective category of thinking that they have internalised after being imposed upon them by those who are currently representing the majoritarian cultural and political system. As Fanon noticed, the spirit of discouragement has been deeply rooted in people's mind by the colonial, which continues to remain on the surface (2011: 156).

In addition, since the post-Eastern Bloc is a region that contains democratic institutions, despite not functioning, minority groups do not need celebration for their national, cultural, or even ethnic identity to offer apt strategies for, or pave the way to, a liberation struggle. It is instead a philosophical, perhaps too critical, approach to reading hegemony and understanding it from within in all its divisive structures of cultural and political power. In addition, a post-colonial paradigm seems to unravel subtler mechanisms through which Communist legacy of power continues to function in the political and cultural realm, going beyond the profound marks left in areas and relations of economy and re-analysing the fabrication of political power and authority in the light of the poorly achieved results of democratic transitions. It has especially marked, and continues to, a profound, albeit general, understanding of being (Maldonado-Torres 2007: 242) through which previous points of reference were translated into new spatio-temporal conditions of democracy.

In addition, it would seem to affirm that such trajectory is much more visible than in the past. To put it simply, the "colonial" – namely, a mechanism of patronising the "Other" and hierarchic doing of politics – mirrors the category of (post-)"socialist". Although coloniality cannot be fully applied (arguably) over post-Communism, it seems to trace the trajectory along which modalities of hegemonic appropriation and externally imposed ascription of societal, political, and cultural features have been kept at work throughout the post-Communist society, thereby empowering certain segments of society rather than initiating a mutual process of empowerment upon "other" cultures and groups. In this, lack of legitimisation and failure of full recognition, accommodation, and integration are manifest in hybrid democratic regimes. In the constant attempt to move forward achievements of full-fledged democracies, the post-Communist subject seems to travel from the future to the past, moving thereby backward, navigating against the movement of the normal flow of time.

Of course, it is important to here clarify that nodal points of reference are not those that have ideologically shaped the region in the aftermaths of the Second World War until 1989/1991. However, at the same time, as Foejtö noticed, the celebrated thesis of the Communist ideology, which aimed at erecting humanity from the ruins of bourgeois society, has not abolished any antagonism between groups, so-called "classes" in Marxist terms. It has instead substituted old classes with new ones, imposed new conditions of oppression in the place of old ones, and new forms of struggle for certain segments of societies rather than one for the whole society (1974: 399). In ahistorical parallel, post-colonial theory can be useful to even turn away from the Marxist political theorists and their economy-related condition of (under)development as a means of fighting the subject affected by colonial and neo-colonial forces. For example, cultural commonalities would seem to confirm how socialist legacy is a surprising model of cultural superiority that continues to culturally function and be politically employed. From a historical point of view, for example, one of the evils of the Stalinist system in the People's Democracies was the despotic attitude of the bureaucracies of ethnically dominant groups towards the numerous minority groups within the framework of national and multinational states, the various constitutions of which stipulated equality of rights of all the nationalities. It was, therefore, not surprising that the revival of nationalism should have provoked a more or less general movement among the minorities, who also asked for a certain degree of administrative, cultural, and even economic autonomy. Tensions, grievances, and conflicts supposedly resolved manifested themselves (Fejtö 1974: 289). It is here interesting to notice how such historical explanation of de-Stalinisation of Eastern Europe seems to have not come to an end, but it still functions through ethnically dominant groups that came out from the hegemonic Communist forces but imposed a similar domination upon numerous minority groups.

However, it is not simply what Fukuyama named "megalothymia", that is, every person's or group's desire to be recognised as superior and powerful and the feeling of resentment that arises when one is disrespected and not publicly recognised for its human worth (2016: 21). It is a much subtler category of thought that has been left working in the region and shaped a form of (post-)coloniality which came to take place in support of ethno-national majoritarian cultural model and subjugate minority cultural claims. As largely explained so far, identity has been a critical issue in the then-socialist world. Similar to Asia, Africa, and Latin America, in which a Western "domination without development" had left more a legacy of cultural weakness than a vacant space for political institutions to develop, in the former Eastern bloc Western values and moral-philosophical principles of democracy have been euphorically introduced without a serious sociopolitical understanding of the region itself. Here, although Socialist colonialism formally ceased to exist due to collapse of the Eastern bloc, coloniality has embedded itself into a "new" form of political thinking and cultural knowing emerging within already-made externally constructed boundaries based on interests of hegemons (Castellino 2018: 344). To simply put it, this approach refers to a "coloniality of being" salient on a cultural level rather than representing a manifesto-like "liberation struggle" on a political one. Applied over the context of minority issues in CEE, a colonising way of thinking (i.e., cultural patronisation) from which "inferiority" and social category of subordination stem from, is being imposed upon certain segments of society. Similar to how Communist regimes had benefitted from a Marxist ideology against sub-nations within a State, such colonising and patronising attitude of the social majority systems has been interiorised, reformulated in the post-1989 epoch, and nowadays still applied for setting respective "others" apart. Again, while the "Communist colonialism" has formally ceased to exist, coloniality began to exercise itself in the democratic life through colonial forms of living and knowing in relation to "ethnic", "gender", "radical", and, to a certain extent, "political" features of minority groups. What "former" national minority cultures suffered from, namely being colonised by the overwhelming ideology of socialism, is today suffered by minority cultures in their post-socialist human condition, whose marginalisation and exclusion has ceased to exclusively represent politically notions of power, but it continues to impose culturally hegemonic position in the public realm. Hence, coloniality is thus nothing but a useful paradigm through which asserting how certain segments of the post-Communist societies and lifeworld have been "colonised" by being systematically set apart from the ethno-majoritarian cultural mechanism of power that does not cease to instrumentally suppress forms of social integration (Habermas 1985: 196, cited by de Geus 2018: 9) rather than others. All of these might have the potential to enter the discussion for a reconsideration of "minority dislocation", which has been so far related to the risk of putting territorial integrity at stake or trigger self-ghettoisation and irredentism after allocating a larger degree of self-governing rights.

This (semi-)colonial environment was felt in the Balkan region throughout the Communist experience. For example in François Fejtö's paragraph devoted to "The Fate of National Minorities" in his *A History of People's Democracies* (1974), the Hungarian-born French political historian recalled Ceausescu's speech given in Sofia, Bulgaria, in 1966. During the event, Communist Romania's leader directly addressed his Bulgarian counterpart to remark how Balkan people, who have historically been quite often the pawns of the imperialist powers in their policy of domination and conquest over the region, have a mutual interest in cooperation. If it is clear the politics-oriented interests by which that speech was delivered, addressing directly Zhivkov and his position on Bulgaria's favourable relations with USSR, it seemed that such idea of being the pawns of imperialist forces has always been haunting across Southeast Europe. Not surprisingly, in both countries, Romania and Bulgaria, the post-Communist transition towards full-fledged democratic regimes occurred after an overwhelming nationalisation of the Communist ideology which began to reinforce, unite, and centralise the national character of the state along the ethno-majoritarian lines. Even before the demise of Communism, this phenomenon began to deteriorate both human condition and societal position of minority groups not only in Bulgaria and Romania but across the whole Eastern Bloc (1974: 289).

All of these do not only concern the essentialist or construct dilemma in understanding minority identities in the wider public. In contrast, the whole debate concerns the critique against those who are reconsidering the possibility to present the experience of the state of socialism as an inspiration or tool for building a more equitable, freer, and peaceful society today (Kušić, Lottholz, and Manolova 2019). It thus contrasts any pitfall of reconsideration of historical experience in Southeast Europe, such as the one that sees the Ottoman experience as the most developed form of the group rights model in terms of religious tolerance (Kymlicka 1992: 38), or the state of socialism in CEE as a model to reconsider in terms of collective coexistence under the umbrella of a shared system of values and practices, social mores, and institutional arrangements, in opposition to the significant tension within the Occidental system (Karkov and Valiavicharska 2018: 791). At the same time, it dissolves the academic approach that scholars continue to use for perpetuating an image of a CEE as a pathological region (Nordstrom 1999, Fassin and Pandolfi 2010), due to which impossibility of achieving a true interethnic coexistence and tolerance affects a transition toward full-fledged democracy and economic development.

If this first part remains general and oriented to build my

argumentation for the further sections, this study employs the notion of coloniality as a category of thinking. The latter plays a centrally paramount role if combined with the poststructuralist scholarship. By definitely moving the discussion from the "essential versus construct" dilemma, it helps to dig into the connection between identity facets of minority groups and their politico-normative issues. Moreover, it seeks to illustrate pre-emerging or newly-fresh nodal points for social activism and related struggles for recognition in the wider public while critically interrogating neo-liberal structuring and internalisation of ethno-essentialist and hegemonic ways of thinking and knowing. In light of the high level of complexities that this approach raises on a philosophical ground, one may agree that although there is a desire to claim poststructuralism as a rupture, the latter is only a repetition (Spivak 1999: 351) with nothing new to offer with respect to precedent philosophical scholarships. However, the latter seems scholarly capable to disentangle numerous possibilities and competing narratives over those multiple identities (co-)existing in parallel or in opposition within one collective Self. It also proves that taking for granted an identity along with an identification to an external object (e.g., an "other") in time and space, as the majority of structuralism scholars maintain, may be wrong. Conversely, the presence of multi-layered identities of an "Other within" (Glavanakova 2016) enables us to best investigate the Self among its own selves. In this, poststructuralism may be understood as a philosophical investment in highlighting alternative modes of liberation — modes that are not necessarily "new", but that bear the traces of non-hegemonic or subaltern thinking, the survival of which evinces simultaneously the constitutive underside of modernity and the possibility of other worlds (Maese-Cohen 2010: 14).

If applied over social categories of "majority versus minority" in post-Communist societies, this approach comes definitely to challenge the classic definitions of culture-oriented patterns. The same notions of such parameters can also be questioned (Ali 2004). At the very end, both carriers of the terms "identity" and "culture" have been cordoned off by philosophy, which has so far policed the same cordons and maintained some distractions in order to prevent at all costs wanderers from stumbling back onto the terrain of future projects (Murray 2018: 224). Because of this, the main goal is to highlight evidence of a wide range of philosophical stances present in the contemporary political arena. For example, among others, the recall for Derrida's act of deconstructing should permit a rough re-evaluation at first, and reexamination at second, of the rigid paradigm by which post-Communist majority-minority relations have been investigated, along with a sociopolitical degree to which political discursive strategies have managed to facilitate an old-fashioned and one-dimensional approach towards minority issues, the majority of which are understood along and from ethnic majoritarian lines.

Paraphrasing Nawaz's understanding of the Muslim community (no matter if majority or minority within the country or region), the latter seems to have certain nuances of Derrida's deconstruction. In particular, Nawaz shows not only a deep degree of intersectional differences among members belonging to the same community, but it also shows how a religious minority is always opened to change (2015: 4).

Through three concentric spaces of cultural identities of Islam, Nawaz notices that the first circle is composed of the smallest and extremely peripheral group, yet best organised and most vocal, within the Muslim community (Nawaz and Harris 2015: 75). Within this, members may be externally influenced by jihadi-movements, such as Islamic State, al-Qaeda, Boko Haram, al-Shebab and so forth. Their potential incitements to war or interethnic enmity, which had found a fertile ground after the Balkan Wars in the 1990s, have been paramount for self-proclaimed pro-jihadi movements and their continuous attempts to target Muslims worldwide. In this circle, disloyal and radical confessional reconstruction have facilitated the already orthodox and straightforward practices of Islam in the realm of everyday life. Although demonisation of infidels, belief in martyrdom, jihad as a way to achieving the holy glory has epistemologically contradicted the moral contents of Quranic prescribed actions, and they have hermeneutically de-sacralised the contents of the sacred Book (Nawaz 2015: 88), this form of religious identity has never ceased to oppose to the West in order to express cultural rejection of liberal values. Moreover, it has never stopped to promote political opposition to the neutral role of the State thanks to an increasing sympathy for separatist movements that have not ceased to gain popularity since the 1970s (Jenkins 2007).

Around this, there is another semi-peripheral and larger circle, the second one, in which the religious identity problem is quite acute. Muslims are here involved in Islam despite the fact that they appear much less eager to misbehave on behalf of Allah and willing to entirely sacrifice themselves for Allah. Within this, Muslims are more oriented towards following and supporting Islam financially, philosophically and morally, but other concepts such as secularism, democracy and reinterpretation of Qur'an appear an assault upon Islam and their identity. In general, these people are extremely conservative in their own families and lifestyle, posing certain core human rights challenges even though they are not willing to impose their religion upon others. In particular, among Muslim women who are part of this circle, the result of the secularisation of Islam in the liberal society is seen through the negative picture of too many broken marriages, women left without the security of their men, and deteriorating relations between men and women (Frog and Orr-Ewing 2002: 65). In other words, the members of this second circle are not inclined to get their hands dirty for or on behalf of Allah. They follow styles of belief and practices that would not flourish under strict or puritanical regime even though they live in accordance with an old-fashioned Islamic tradition.

In the end, there is yet another community space, that is, a third circle, the broadest and the largest, which is composed of those non-observant "cultural Muslims" (Jenkins 2010, 122) to whom it unconsciously happened to be Muslims. In Western and Southeast Europe in general, or in Bulgaria, France or Germany in particular, they represent the majority of those involved either in today's campaigns for political and cultural recognition within Christian-majoritarian cultural systems where Christian values and practices are widespread (e.g., Bulgaria, North Macedonia, Serbia, Greece), or engaged in processes of policy-making aimed at "sharing religions to shape Nations" (e.g., Bosnia and Herzegovina, Albania and Kosovo). Despite the fact that sometimes they do not possess a secular looking, they do not straightforwardly practise Islam in its orthodoxy, nor they are in agreement with pro-jihadi propaganda within and above Muslim communities they belong to. Interestingly enough, they possess a very low understanding of Islam as a whole, of its sacred texts of Qur'an, and Arabic fluency is generally lacking or is oftentimes very poor. However, they belong to families and communities living in closed marginal, or spatially peripheral, milieus that offer a localised, oftentimes hybrid or idiosyncratic, form of Islam. Nowadays, despite the fact that they distance themselves from old-fashioned ways of family life, time of social insecurity and uncertainty for the future brought them to a religious throwback to Islam and its paraphernalia, rigid beliefs and orthodox practices. This self-identification represents an island of stability and certainty in their eyes (Jenkins 2007: 155), even though certain family features continue to be rejected, such as the division between men and women based on a patriarchal ideology that very much determines how the whole Muslim community is generally structured. Because of this, it would be possible to redefine these "new Muslims" from the third circle as "Muslims-by-choice" despite the fact they are anything but religious in any approved or institutionalised regime. Their self-identification and alignment with Islam do not follow those of their parents, the majority of whom is often found in support of a culture that "Muslims-by-choice" have never seen as their in the present-day. At the same time, they are afraid to tell their parents that they have lost their faith in Allah, for fear of being ostracised by them (Nawaz 2015: 73). They know that in their early years they have "Westernised" themselves for having conducted and kept a lifestyle similar to that of the people equal in age.

Although they account for a large segment of an autochthonous Muslim population in Southeast Europe, or second generation Muslims in Western Europe, their "being Muslim" simply refers to a set of social practises and moral rules that they traditionally follow more in the private sphere rather than in the public one. These "non-observant Muslims", which Jenkins names as "cultural Muslims" (Jenkins 2007:122), represent apparently a familiar type. Within this circle, "being a Muslim" takes the form of an idiosyncratic identity. The term "idiosyncratic" recalls its literally Greek origin: "idiosunkrasia" in its trifold meaning: "idios" (ἴδιος) "own" or "private", which brings to light a self-identification with Islam among Balkan Muslims that is acquired in the private sphere (e.g. family, madrasas, mosques, civic organisations, charitable associations and so on); sun (σύν) "with", namely the "bridge" with all aspects of Balkan Muslim population mentioned above; "krasis" (κρᾶσις) – "mixture" – which comes to lay out a wide range of cultural, linguistic, ethnic, historical and political facets of today's form of Islam in Southeast Europe. In other words, this idiosyncratic identity of "being Muslim" is tied and more likely subordinated to a soft-identity that lacks a serious and well-defined understanding of boundaries related to cultural, religious and political patterns in the realm of private as well as public everyday life. Because of this, it is seriously difficult and theoretically challenging to come up with a common definition of the "cultural identity" in Southeast Europe.

Interestingly enough, in the past few years this so-called "idiosyncratic identity" has partially succeeded to influence the "third group" but it has also maintained the Balkan Peninsula disentangled from a deep Islamist and jihadist intrusion. Along with local security actions and international intelligence that have truncated processes of radicalisation, radical form of Islamic identity has never shaped an extreme form of escapism from the social reality. In fact, a high level of self-consciousness among "cultural Muslims" with regards to their minority status, has triggered a softer form of self-identification with radical Islam or complete refusal of externally imposed "identity building".

While "outside confessional (re-)constructions" have been built upon such volatile form of Muslim identity that members have decided to accept to tackle a wealth of misconceptions, stereotypes and discrimination, others have refused to. In this instance, marginalised position in society and phenomena of ghettoisation trigger more self-segregation and antisocial behaviour on behalf of a "cultural authenticity" and "cultural protection". This potential idea may bring Muslims to increase a sense of reflexive solidarity with other Muslim brothers and sisters – no matter how barbaric their commitment might be – and satisfy (unconsciously) religious leaders' aspirations accordingly.

For all of these intersectional aspects, it is important to bear in mind that such philosophy-backed argumentations shall question the issues of minority cultural identities from their own perspective. For example, considering the case study of the "Bulgarian Muslims", which could be easily juxtaposed to Nawaz's deconstructive suggestion, the post-colonial may provide an opportunity to break the stereotypes of colonially constructed binaries and dismantle the whole constructivist philosophy of the "alien other" and its instrumentalist astray. The deconstruction of its rigid association and narrow confinement to competitive mode of construction will generate a new space for neglected and submerged groups to assert their voice and their identity (Karim and Anjum 2016: 41). In this regard, despite the fact that a hostile language against Muslims and Turkish communities is constantly winning ground in Bulgaria (Emilova 2017: 127) and lack of interethnic well-living in contested societies such as in Bosnia and Herzegovina and Kosovo are major concerns, Islam is mistakenly represented as a basic, "demonic" factor. In fact, such religious belief system has been only exposed to interest-oriented influences that can easily escalate, weaken or pacify conditions of (in-)stabilities. Because of this, forms of essentialisation and primordialist views related to the violent nature of Islam should be definitely stopped. According to Meyer's definition of Islam, the latter is a religion able to exalt or intensify the passions and the fury of two, or even more, opposed sides (2002: 210). Most of the time, Islam becomes a mask, one of a symbolic identity-related signifier to use along with its ambiguous paraphernalia in order to hide the real issues at stake. By looking beneath the parapet of the externally imposed discourse over Islam, for instance, an array of intolerant forms or theoretically-driven practical impossibility to establish interfaith relations are presented in our contemporary societies. Within this, an ongoing struggle of power (Meyer 2002) embraces Islam through a specific discourse throughout society. Oftentimes, common nodal points of such discourse and emphasis go on a radical interpretation of infidelity, which is considered the worst deviation from the good life. As Nawaz correctly notices, this interpretation has not been historically foreign to other religions, such as Judaism and Christianity (2015: 83).

In this regards, Bulgaria's Muslim communities have never played a critical role in society even though their religious identity tends to exalt concerns in the wider public. It is only possible to notice that while Islam per se has never created an oasis of persistent hatred and violence as some continue to portray it (Velikonja 2003), at the same time such religious identity has barely built up an oasis of peace, tolerance, and comprehension between different ethnic groups on the Balkans. Perhaps even more clearly, it seems obvious that the transnational essence of Islam and its hybrid form of emphasising how the issues of Balkan Muslim minorities are no longer different from those present in Western Europe, which, for a matter of fact, are post-colonial Nations. After all, from an external perspective, the term "Muslim" is quite misleading. The latter, in general, is shorthand in Europe for a member of an ethnic community established in the second half of the twentieth century and drawn from African to Asian nations where Islam represents the default religion (Jenkins 2007: 155).

In this regard, Piro Rexhepi notes that the "Europeanising project" has been involved in constant attempts to separate Balkan Muslims from the rest of the Muslim world (2018) and that the interconnectedness between Western and Eastern Europe does not really make sense anymore. The latter, which cannot be considered a periphery of Europe, but a crucially cultural region of Europe itself, shows how Muslim communities have shifted from hegemonic to unprivileged positions throughout the ebbs and flows of recent history: from the rise of the Ottoman Empire to its collapse, from the early age of the post-Ottoman period up until to the Communist takeover, since the 1989 and today's cultural dilemma of the Western or Eastern Europe's Muslims.

For example in the recent Bulgarian history, one might easily argue that a form of factual colonisation toward Muslim minorities did not begin in the last period of the Communist period (1984-1989) where the ruling élites attempted to awake a Socialist consciousness among the Turkish minority (Merdjanova 2006), the majority of whom Muslim believers. The societal role of Islam was perceived even before the 1980s as an overwhelming obstacle for the Bulgarian State. The cruel pages of Communist Bulgaria's policies of assimilation and transformation of Muslim identities continued to face troubles with the same Turkish minority members (750,000, or 10 per cent of the population) due to their refusal to be ideologically assimilated. Since 1951, 154,000 ethnic Turks from Dobroudja were repatriated in Turkey, but since then Ankara, unable to absorb these newcomers, shut its gates along with one of the most debated borders of the Eastern Bloc. To a certain extent, the majority of Turks living in Communist Bulgaria were not much irritated by the anti-Turkic press campaign, such as the one by *Rabotnichesko Delo*'s targeting Islam and Turkey as perilous entities for the country. They were basically found resistant against the idea to accept land collectivisation, which was imposed upon their lands through propaganda to which they managed to remain immune. By living in remote rural areas, the Turkish peasantry resisted accepting Bulgaria as their country of ancestral origin while renouncing the Turkish nationality at the same time. Within this, rather than a religious affair, Islam was only used as a leading-threat instrument against the Communist state in order to hide the real political purposes and real power concerns (Fejtö 1974: 295). In fact, only between 1984 and 1989, the Communist regime attempted to forcibly change the identity of Bulgarian Turks by giving them a Slavonic "ethnic code" through an anti-Turkish policy. The former was carried out, according to newly discovered documents, because of a potential Cyprus-like crisis in Southern Bulgaria that pan-Turkic and pro-Turkey nationalists had started to conduct against the civil population (Baev 2015: 169). Justified by the rumour of this potential turmoil, Communist ruling élites used this momentum to begin another campaign against non-Bulgarian citizens. They were forced to change their original names into new and "more Bulgarian" ones, and convinced to have Bulgarian roots as well as descendants and family connections they had lost due to the Ottoman domination (Marinov 2017: 74). This period, which was termed the "Great Revival", provoked yet another mass-scale migration flow of 350,000 Bulgarian-Turks (of whom about 100,000 later returned to Bulgaria) in the direction of Turkey, damaging Bulgaria's name and reputation in the wider Muslim world. Moreover, state confiscations of the property of charitable foundations (e.g., *waqfs*), reduction of the number of functioning mosques and persecution of religious leaders (Merdjanova 2006) took place throughout the collapse of Communist Eastern Bloc regimes, as ideology and political system, while increasing Bulgarians' hostility and mistrust toward ethnic minority groups.

According to this historical case study, whether one might try to combine the category of post-Communist with that of post-Colonial, Rexhepi is beyond doubt a serious point of reference. He in fact argues that trying to differ the story of Balkan Islam from those of the religious beliefs, such as Christianity or Judaism, means to overlook the historical timeline along which Islam has been cyclically silenced by quasi-colonialising nationalist struggles and narratives that, in their turn, have sought to place Balkan Muslim outside their non-Oriental picture of Europe in general, and the region in particular.

Recalling once again Kundera's search for the Western essence of Central Europe during the Communist experience, hence it follows that uniqueness of a certain State's identity has been mistakenly researched against the differences between different locations instead of consequences of power (Quijano 2004: 542). For example, it sounds paradoxical how Max Weber described the power structure of the Ottoman Empire as a "sultanism", thereby refusing the idea of an oppressing empire administration against minority cultures of today's Ottoman successor States, while exposing his anti-Polish rhetoric through an unmistakable colonial logic by which German citizenship appeared the only way to turn the Polish minority in Eastern Prussia into human beings. To a certain extent, what Weber stated did not change over time. Post-socialist discourse and policies have most significantly manifested in ethno-nationalist campaigns of forced assimilations of ethnic and religious minorities whose members have been subjected to new citizenship regime by the new State. According to Boatča, these regimes of contested (e.g., post-Soviet self-proclaimed breakaway republics), sometimes parallel (e.g., Kosovo Serbs), citizenship regimes are the result of an "entail of colonial property", which is most poignantly captured in the contemporary trend of "citizenship by investment" programmes (mentioned by Kušić et al. 2019).

Therefore, on the one hand, the proposed theory of the "coloniality of being" has been criticised for having failed to construct an alternative outside of the Western reference (Mignolo 2007, mentioned in Kušić, Lottholz, and Manolova 2019). On the other hand, however, particularly in Southeast European countries, and more generally in the peripheries of Eastern Europe, critiques of local marginalisation and dispossession are too often based on an identification with Europe rather than on analyses of how these regimes of oppression are globally connected. However, others have argued that the centrality of this philosophical enquiry is to pose the question that was used worldwide for the whole territory of the defunct East of Europe. This recently scholarly theory of the "coloniality of being" offers to the sphere of Minority Studies a better, and critical, angle of investigation over the issues of domination, oppression, and exploitation in CEE. To put it simply, it aims to deconstruct post-socialist subjectivity—no matter if majoritarian or minoritarian—so that it can acknowledge its colonising and colonised positions as well as its anti-colonial legacy in order to offer another, perhaps entirely new, starting point for future projects in academia and praxis. Because of this, different facets of minority issues shall be disentangled through the key relations that have emerged, and continue to, along the binary of post-socialist and post-colonial.

In conclusion, questioning the relation between the post-socialist and the post-colonial in reference to minority subjectivities in Southeast and Eastern Europe through a constantly imposed majoritarian approach of "group antagonism" along with cultural, ethnic, gender, or class notions, would seem to be wrongly conducted nowadays. Only by stepping back, inside the hegemonic structures of the post-socialist European nation states, it is possible to disentangle culturally imposed forms of ascriptions and further political exclusion in the region. Thereby, paraphrasing the above-mentioned Rexhepi's work, the main enquiry to refer to in the second part of this study will be: *how* to speak, and *who* speaks, in the name of the post-socialist minority subjects?

PART II: THE MAKING AND THE RE-MAKING OF SUBALTERNS: A GRAMSCIAN PERSPECTIVE

"The forces operating in history are not controlled by destiny
or regulative mechanisms, but respond to haphazard conflicts.
They do not manifest the successive forms of a primordial intention
and their attraction is not that of a conclusion,
for they always appear through a singular randomness of events"

Michel Focault,
Nietzsche, Genealogy and History (1971)

CHAPTER FOUR

Antonio Gramsci and Subaltern Cultures: Fundamental Remarks

When in the second half of the '80s, the British cultural anthropologist Stuart Hall raised provocatively the following question: "Who needs him for the great diversity of human beings and their ethnic cultural claims that must enter in our world in the 21st century?" (1987: 1-19), "him"[1] referred to the philosophical figure of Antonio Gramsci (1891-1937), one of the top representatives of the European Marxism and a "curious" thinker (Stepanyan 2016: 80). Hence, following Hall's perspective on the relevance of Gramscian legacy in the history of Continental Philosophy, this second part is devoted to Gramsci's philosophical contribution. For the purpose of this study, the so called Theory of Hegemony is methodologically employed by keeping a specific perspective that from below (emic) aims, in turn, to shed light on minority issues in CEE. By doing so, from now on, the term "subaltern" replaces "minority" to give credit to Gramsci's specific terminology, perhaps too slippery, yet worth introducing because used at first by the Italian Marxist (Braeunlien 2014: 3).

By eschewing Gramsci's philosophy of praxis in tandem with a postcolonial approach and other Marxist hindsights, introductory remarks about Gramsci's array of philosophical concepts are needed in order to clarify both political and cultural interconnectedness between (hegemonic) power structure and (subaltern) group identities, and the proposed post-colonial paradigm. Without any doubt, such perspective does not guarantee us to own the keys and further solve identity issues concerning minority groups in our contemporary societies. It is a scholarly attempt to "rethink aloud" about some of the most controversial issues of minority groups in light of, and from the perspective of, Antonio Gramsci's philosophical contribution and sociophilosophical legacy. Moreover, the post-colonial paradigm is thus employed to examine to what extent post-socialist minority subjects can

---

[1] Stuart Hall spent quite lot of time to re-read Gramsci and his Prison Notebooks in search of a more adequate account for Marxism. See more, Stuart Hall. Gramsci's Relevance for the Study of Race and Ethnicity, in: Journal of Communication Inquiry, Vol. 10, No. 2, 1986: 24.

speak and are (not) able to formulate their claims into a space of safe existence. Although the post-colonial paradigm has been so far used as a quintessentially political or historical concept, the trajectory of so-called coloniality may be employed to investigate the interpenetration of knowledge and power in the postCommunist CEE. Within the Gramscian framework, in turn, the post-colonial paradigm would potentially be seen as one of the vectors of study of minority issues, thereby extending the scholarly trajectory of post-colonial theory toward a "third stage" in the wake of Edward W. Said's Orientalism (1978), Michael Foucault's discursive analysis, Jacques Derrida's theory of deconstruction and Spivak's question "Can Subaltern Speak?" (1988).

In all of these, which are key to the main point of this study, it shall be highlighted and discovered anew the very fabric of post-Communist "colonialism".

Nevertheless, it is worth drawing attention to a few notes of caution with respect to potential misunderstanding that might be revealed from my decision to deal with Gramsci's uncanny insight and slippery terminology of his "curious" Marxism. Although Gramsci's account is based on different cases related to the Italian State and society, his analysis of the category of hegemony and condition of subalternity may better unravel the historical "organic crisis" in Communist Europe, thereby stirring issues of minority groups in different times and spaces than those where Gramsci lived. While the curious Marxist wrote very little about racism and colonialism, his Sardinian youth certainly acquainted him with uneven development and the lived realities of semicolonial rules (Blackburn 2014: 84). In fact, he was always sensitive to questions of cultural differences, speaking up for the "Southern Question" in Italy and the subaltern role of the peasantry and its societal implications (e.g. peasantinism) after the 1861 unification of Italy and its modern statehood development. He had stirred up questions about the Ottoman Armenian struggle for survival and claims to land against the pan-Turkic nationalism on the verge of the Ottoman Empire collapse. He had paid attention to the Serb hegemonic forces stopping rural reforms in the Kingdom of Yugoslavia. He had also noticed how subtly and implicitly certain mechanisms of American expansionism would have used Afro (subaltern) communities in America to conquer the African market and secure the extension of the American civilisation worldwide (Gramsci 1971, quoted in Spivak 1999: 376). Perhaps inevitable for the personal profile of an intellectual, Antonio Gramsci, whose father's family descended from Arbëreshë Christians who settled in Southern Italy in the fifteenth century following the Ottoman occupation of the Balkan Peninsula, always expressed an unequivocal empathy for the oppressed, the neglected and the deprived, as all orthodox Marxists did.

At the same time, however, Gramsci's philosophical contribution has been largely misunderstood and misinterpreted because of his political implication with the Communist Party of Italy and his theorisation of the radical liberation of the "working class". In this regard, many have tried to fit and harmonise Gramsci's philosophy of praxis into a specific political discourse or theoretically formulate it into a new horizon of interdisciplinary field of research, such as critical sociology, cultural anthropology, gender studies, media studies, and so forth. Others tried instead to justify his slippery terminology by attempting to coherently explain the Gramscian emancipatory vocabulary within one of the academic silos related to structuralism or poststructuralism scholarship. As a matter of fact, both attempts have generally achieved very little. They have been instead exposed to several critiques in academia and beyond, leaving at the same time space for new interpretation of how Gramsci's notion of hegemony along with categories of culture and ideology have been philosophically appealing but misleading too.

One of the most common pitfalls that (arguably) resulted from attempts to deal with Antonio Gramsci's legacy is related to the philosophically chaotic, oftentimes politically biased, interpretation of his philosophical contribution under the umbrella of post-modernism. To a certain extent, Gramsci's work may largely sound post-modern in accordance with his sociological explanations of the complexities and paradoxes of hegemonic structures and agency in the social realm. In particular, Gramsci had pointed out much earlier than the development of post-modernism that individual as well as collective identities and social groups along with their social behaviour patterns are constantly subject to political and cultural transformations along contingent roads of constant becoming due to same transformations that upper hegemonic driving forces dictate throughout society. Ideologies organise in turn masses and create a terrain on which they move, acquiring consciousness of their position, and struggling accordingly (Gramsci 1971: 377). To a certain extent, a "poststructuralist Gramsci" may reflect his existential idea to elaborate on what one really is "knowing thyself". This may be the product of historical processes to date, which have deposited in the Self an affinity of traces, yet without an inventory for explaining certain conditions of existence. Therefore, it is imperative at the outset to compile an inventory, among a genealogy of subjects or objects, part of a necessary condition for understanding the real—which is to say historical (Cohen 2018: 6). Besides, many others have pointed out that contradictory interpretations of Gramsci's philosophy partly derive from such particular "poststructuralist interpretation" of his thoughts, which force the figure of Gramsci to have become a participant in a debate that opposes structure to the agency, and vice versa (Ciovolella 2013). In this case, a poststructuralist analysis over the Gramscian legacy cannot be an article of faith, but a resource in the field of phenomenology or political ontology.

In this regard, Gramsci's critical approach to societal power and cultural structures cannot be reduced to only the conviction that "Marx was right, but that Marxist theory itself has to be completed" (Gordon 1997: 70, mentioned by Rabaka 2009: 280). Following what Laclau made clear (Marchart 2018: 19), a certain degree of deconstruction is necessary to move forward toward a more completed analysis of minority issues, which are in need to be completed by a Theory of Hegemony in the attempt to deconstruct an undecidable terrain (Laclau 1996: 66-83). Yet, if hence we confront Gramsci with historically orthodox interpretation of Karl Marx's philosophy or Marx himself, we take correctly for granted that Antonio Gramsci has surely given a central place to the questions of "class", "class alliances", and "class struggle". Once again, there are no doubts that Gramsci himself belongs to the Marxian ideological conviction of the "Working Class", namely the "Great Proletariat". However, while none has so far clucked up the active engagement of the Sardinian philosopher from such revolutionary tradition, we have to confront quite remarkable differences with the philosophical tradition Gramsci belongs to. For instance, the Italian philosopher is well-known for having been a determined opponent of economic determinism. In this regard, among others, his usage of the term "class" does not really follow the Marxist trajectory. In Gramsci's language, in fact, "class" refers largely to "*ceto*" rather than "*classe*", which literally loses its Italian meaning once translated into English in reference to the term "class". In addition, the particular nuance that the "class" and its "struggle" have in Gramscianism have to be considered as transcending the particularities of their objectives and tending to establish, thereby impose, a much larger and widespread "common sense" that leads the whole society toward an universal praxis for social justice and recognition. As Gramsci himself had noticed, "ceto" and "classe" are not the same societal entity. Given this token, in his Theory of Hegemony Gramsci preferred *ceto* rather than *classe*, particularly specifying how a given "class" — or a cluster of individuals represented or to be represented under the banner of "class" — is not a concrete and objective entity. It instead comes into existence in the political realm as well as the cultural one as a constitutive entity coming into being because of the ideological practice of the system (Cheskin 2016: 150). Relatedly, the Gramscian use of the term "subaltern" with regard to the notion of "class" brought a group of scholars to adhere to the so-called "censorship thesis" – namely, the assumption that Gramsci referred to "Proletariat" with the term "subaltern", and, by the same token, to "communism" with the definition of "philosophy of praxis", as codewords for strategically avoiding prison censorship. For instance, Gayatri Chakravorty Spivak claimed so in 1992, affirming that "subaltern" is a term with a description of a military thing, used by Gramsci on purpose (1992). However, this thesis can be easily rejected as a general analysis of the Prison Notebooks reveals no indication that Gramsci devised or used code-words or even euphemisms, with both terms appearing throughout the text (Green 2011). This perspective posed a challenge to the essentialist conception of class in the work of Marx and Marxist thinkers. For instance, Gramsci's focus on the non-hegemonic roles of peasantry and intellectuals under the hegemonic forces of the working class and the party in society gave recent popularity to Gramsci among liberation movements in the post-colonial period in the Global South. What Gramsci had contributed was a partial abandonment of Marx's "class struggle", which began to be seen as stereotypically restless in its potentially deriving results—fatalism. Aimed at awakening a new man-oriented *socium* (in Italian: *Uomo Nuovo*) for a better society to come, Gramsci pointed out how hegemonic structures shape a *homo oeconomicus* whose transformation and realisation depends on the parallel transformation of the society, namely, the transformation of the civil society at first. As Spivak noted by quoting Gramsci, a potential revolution will inevitably bring a new mode of production and a collective economic behaviour accordingly (1999: 83). It thus follows that Marxist interpretation of culture, which results from ideological imposition of the ruling class, is slightly different in Gramsci. According to Gramsci indeed, culture owns the awakening force and teleological mission *for interesting us, for moving us* [to know] *something* [that must be] *recognisable, which must affect a people of whom we have heard spoken before, and who thus belongs to our circle of humanity"*[2]. As Gramsci largely pointed out, perhaps by revising Marx's category of culture, indifference is the dead weight of history, and culture is for knowing existential conditions (Spivak 1999: 270), particularly for those who do not pay heed (Gramsci 1971: 191).

It also followed that the philosophical pillar of Gramsci's contribution to Marxism took a different path from the orthodoxy of Marxism itself. In a few words, yet centrally paramount to be clarified, the Theory of Hegemony does not only, and directly, relate to the exclusive categories

---

[2] An allusion to Gramsci's article "Armenia 1915", written for "Il Grido del Popolo" [The Shout of the People] dated March 11, 1916.

of power and authority. Rather, it mainly deals with parallel domination of knowledge as (colonial) instrument of reconciliation throughout a "passive revolution" (e.g., "revolution-restoration"), which Gramsci used as a standard analysing tool. By doing so, he philosophically replaced the Marxist desire to dissolve society through a non-mediated action of liberation. As explained below in detail, potential misunderstanding might come from a long-term, highly misleading translation of the same category of hegemony within the Marxist tradition. In the aftermath of the Second World War, the term "hegemony" has been translated into Italian and Russian languages mainly in terms of "*direzione*" for the first and "*rukovodstvo*" (in Russian: руководство) for the second. Strictly speaking, both terms do not refer literally to a kind of hegemonic domination or imposition; they do both refer instead to the term "leadership" (English translation) which gives yet another impression of "hegemony" if applied according to Gramsci's philosophy as a whole. In fact, Gramsci was (un-)expectedly able to put under focus the notion of power not only in terms of hegemony. Looking beneath the façade of power (e.g., institutions, law, politics, and so on) the nature of power in-itself is not only ideologically or economically constructed, but also related to moral, intellectual, cultural, and sexual questions of identity. According to Gramsci, identity largely results from the hegemonic exercise of the ideological domination of one class over the subaltern segments of society, which includes a mastery over the people's "common sense" (Selden 1988: 455). From the latter is possible to validate a social behaviour whose commonly accepted identity patterns are negotiated in that very realm (Gramsci 1971). In other words, what people think, who they think they are, and how they socially behave have to fit such "common sense", that is, in the very end, a set of externally imposed ethical and societal values that social beings obey in contingent time and space. Aware of the potential pitfalls that such scholarly orientation might bring out, I do not aim to reinterpret Gramsci's insights over the rules and norms of a society. After all, Gramsci's philosophy cannot be completely decontextualized from his personal experience of imprisonment and the historical epoch in which he lived. Nor does it seem correct to undermine, or not pay attention to, his philosophical and political devotion to the cause of the "Proletarian movement" and the Communist Party he himself founded in Livorno, Italy, in 1921. Nevertheless, Gramsci's legacy has so far shown how his whole philosophical contribution cannot be narrowed solely down into the field of "Marxology" and its orthodox interpretation. Perhaps too provocative, by confronting Gramsci and Marx, we can highlight different points of divergence. Therefore, certain categories openly derive not only from the Marxist tradition, but also from the Hegelian ones, in between which Gramsci philosophically navigated (Laclau 2000: 47). As a result of all of these, it is not my goal to point out a potential reinterpretation of Gramsci's philosophy of praxis, nor to try to reread, to reinterpret, or to reinvent his contribution in accordance with a structuralist or a poststructuralist overview. On the contrary, his idea of "organic crisis" seems applicable in the post-1989 era with regard to minority groups' positionality. Hence, the category of hegemony, which must be understood as a form of leadership, relates to a mutually interwoven form of power and culture, which are in turn not excluded from the moment of deconstruction and new construction of the realm, if and only if they lead to something new (Hall 1987). Finally, yet another crucial aspect is the societal role of minority group intellectuals, which are seen as a collective of subaltern owners of knowledge in the terrain of the civil society, which Gramsci opposed to the State's leadership and discourse.

CHAPTER FIVE

1989 "Organic Crisis" and Post-Communist Positionality of Minority Groups

Happy is the country, George Eliot wrote, *that has no history. By extension, unhappy are the Balkans* [and other regions in the former Communist orbit[1]] *that have too much* (Winchester 1999: 35). From a minority perspective, the aftermath of the Communist collapse meant nothing but a historic opportunity to get the momentum for healing wounds of past disgraces. Three decades onwards, there is still a lively debate about the causes which brought the Communist experience to end in the former Eastern Bloc. For a long time, the *"annus mirabilis"*, the 1989 (Ahrens 2007: 536), was seen as constitutive momentum where the stone of democracy was about to be built on the ruins of the previous regimes. Many have focussed on the rise of ethno-nationalistic forces that began to destabilize from within the entire Communist region as one of the most obvious consequences of a long period of openness (e.g., glasnost, perestroika) that after Joseph Stalin's death in 1953 exposed Communism to global factors and pressure of international actors. Others base their thesis on internally visible economic declines and their inevitable further consequences. In general, much time and effort have been devoted to give lucid analysis of both structural and agential conditions leading one of the largest socio-political experiments in the history of humankind to a complete dissolution. In between, scholars and academics have recently started to propose yet another explanation for looking beneath events that anticipated the symbolic collapse of the Berlin Wall in 1989 and continue to affect the region since then.

 This newly-fresh perspective lies in the philosophical foundation of Antonio Gramsci's Theory of Hegemony in general, and the notion of "organic crisis" in particular, both shedding light on genealogic moments of an ideological apparatus that grips over a new emerging model of social life, when the old is about to die and the new cannot be born (op. cit., 1971). Without any doubt, the historical period Gramsci lived in, and suffered from, cannot be minimally compared either

---

[1] For the post-Soviet Caucasian region see more Rouben Galichian "The Clash of Histories. Redrawing the Map of Azerbaijan, Armenia and Iran", London: Bennet & Bloom, 2012.

politically or culturally with the overall atmosphere and peculiar contingencies that weakened Communist CEE at the end of the Communist era. However, as many have pointed out (Laclau and Mouffe 1985; Cheskin 2016, among others), Gramsci's philosophical as well as sociological insights are here useful for successfully confronting the nodal (structural) points around which the stucco façade democratic rules of the post-Communist democracies came to function. In order to grasp the large variety of problems and issues that minority groups and their collective identities embarked in CEE, what we can first and foremost identify is a set of cultural and political movements in motion, interlinked and not chronologically separated in different phases of human history. Perhaps, the demise of the Communist era in CEE is graspable through the prism of the "organic crisis". After the overwhelming but short-lived euphoria for the fall of the Berlin Wall, the demise of Communism deserves to be investigated through the study of numerous group identity formations, peoplehood and taxonomy coalescing around national and/or neglected identities (Cheskin 2016:150). While history is scholarly defined as the summary of humanity's past and written from a single perspective that largely overlooks microhistories among cultures, disciplines, and peoples, Gramsci's "organic crisis" enables the understanding of lasting operational functions through which identity-forming nodal points come into play as fixations of ascription to certain segments of society rather than others and from which societal positionality derives. Therefore, the "organic crisis" cannot be simply understood in itself as a breakdown, one of no return of a historical period. Instead, it is the fundamental condition that is constituted by the lasting possibility given to an emerging group (e.g. historical bloc) to come to power – namely, to become hegemonic by imposing a new ideology. Such newly-formed ideology, which is already on the raise along with, and thanks to, the emerging group, imposes a new direction in social life, out of which different identities and their groups will be (dis-)placed accordingly.

Given this token, the "1989 annus mirabilis" cannot be reduced to a chronological summary of historical events, decisions, treaties, struggle and so forth. It has to be seen beneath traditional history, that is, a reversal of relationship of forces, usurpation of power, and the entrance of a masked "other" (Foucault 1971: 154-155). Following such perspective, economics-related explanation of any crisis meant for Gramsci nothing but a partial condition of the collapse and the pre-emerging nucleus of what he referred as hegemony, or, more appropriately, of "hegemonic bloc". Thus, the historical demise of the Communist experience cannot be only seen through an exclusively political or/and economic explanation of the deterioration caused by both national and international factors, which, interplaying mutually, moved on toward a disaster[2]. While scholars tend to underline that such collapse could not have happened without a political turmoil that occurred within a "leading-nation", others point conversely out that the collapse did happen because of a much larger, and deeper, deterioration of those subaltern, cultural and political forces that a nation is composed of, which came across local and world-wide fields (Gramsci 1971: 350). Throughout, the role of collective identities and their positionality in the realm have a central role in time of an "organic crisis". Once the latter shifts gears, the previous apparatus is already into a pre-emerging condition throughout which various political and cultural hegemonic bloc is in struggle to emerge, leading itself to come into being, and manifesting itself by coming to power (Gramsci's momentum toward dominance).

This (pre-)moment is first and foremost a period of deconstruction but at the same time mutually interwoven with the beginning of a new phase of (re-)construction. To a certain extent, a post-colonial read of the collapse of Communism in the former Eastern Bloc might focus on the role of cultures and communities which in the form of (national) minorities came to destabilise Moscow-centralised political and cultural organisation by shaping a new discourse of existences. Three decades onward, discursive identity strategies have largely shown the construction of new discourses of existence. The cases of the Latvian struggle during the Soviet administration, and of ethnic Albanians in Kosovo prior to the 1999 Kosovo War, are both instructive. In the first case, Atmoda (i.e., the Awakening), the official newspaper of the Popular Front of Latvia, covered the oppressive actions of the party by supporting the liberation discourse through Vladimir Lenin's position on "The Rights of Nations and Self-Determination" (Lenin 1972: 393-454). Against Stalin and Brezhnev's national policy, Atmoda reused Lenin's principles against the Soviet oppression, which had forcibly transformed Latvians into a minority in their own country (Cheskin 201: 48–50). In the second case, the Kosovo Albanian discourse against the Serbian-oriented Yugoslavian hegemony was discredited by the same Belgrade-centred power structure through a paradoxical definition of the Albanian claims as the face-saving liaison composed of Islamic fundamentalism and Enver Hoxha's Marxism-Leninism in Albania

---

[2] From now on, the term "disaster" follows the astrological meaning that Gramsci had noticed: a composed name of "dis"-"aster", namely the "fall" of an "aster", a star, which recalls the pictorial decadence of a "shooting star". As Gramsci pointed out: "nobody today thinks that the word "dis-aster" is connected with astrology or can claim to be misled about the opinions of someone who uses the word." (Gramsci 1971, op. cit.).

(Mahmuti 2015: 395). As GM Tamás clearly explains, among the pivotal factors that brought the Communist regime in CEE to collapse there was that of (re-)using the ideology and revolutionary discourse of Marxism outside the hierarchic methods trough which central power kept people at check and ruled over. Venturing the parapet of the Marxist rhetoric of Communist regime, as in the Soviet Union as in Yugoslavia, meant an appropriation of the same revolutionary discourse of Marxism and discomfort for the party members in power those days (Tamás 2009: 35).

In both examples, particularly in the Latvian one, according to what Gramsci noticed, in order to gain power, it is necessary to enjoy elements of hegemony. In this, appropriation of a vocabulary to be turned against those who had once use it (Focault 1971: 157) was beyond doubt an important strategy to speak the truth in front of the power hierarchies and cease the previous usage of that type of rhetoric. This form of enjoyment of hegemonic elements, despite being carried out into a subaltern (or minority) position, has to be performed through activities oriented to gain consensus. The latter literally means, in Gramsci's terms, that the creation of a new hegemony through a leading operation shapes a counter-hegemonic consent to be at first organised in the realm of everyday life (Gramsci 1971). In this regard, Atmoda's anti-hegemony discursive strategy shows how a discourse of existence arose from within the Soviet hegemony, through nodal points which were well-established in the power and cultural structures. The Latvian and Kosovar cases confirm Gramsci's presupposition and similarities: two socialist countries "under fire" and threatened by the same ideological discourse they were based on. Similarly, a historical perspective can even shed light on how Lenin's political strategy of mobilisation was directed to an engagement of the nationalist forces present in the Tsarist Russia, to be turned against the same Romanov dynasty (Nałęcz 2018: 1). As Feijtö had noted, national revival in CEE has in the "first place" taken the form of a return to national indigenousness along traditional, historical, and original belonging lines, which destabilised the Communist hegemonic structures and their hierarchic methods of doing politics in the sphere of everydayness immediately after the death of Joseph Stalin in 1953. Since then, the further period of openness (e.g., glasnost) paved the way to a further period of recognition and struggles resulted from leaders' willingness to secure power position by all possible means (Kushnir 2018: 137). In fact, in the "second place" of the "long 1953", parties, governments, and diverse populations of People's Republics began to call for justice and recognition for the bloodthirsty Stalinist period of mass-deportation, executions, and violence. Nevertheless, the feminist thinker Madina Tlostanova considers the entire period of Soviet "openness" nothing but another period of colonisation, one of much subtler control of power and discourse in which people were once again undergoing a new process of subordination despite the fact that they had assumed the new realm a bit freer and more open to differences[3].

What was more likely a cultural reaction on several levels of the Communist society: behaviour and ideology of the Communist leaderships, multinational interstate relations between internal republics or satellite states, and, finally, the position of minority groups in these countries (Feijtö 1974: 271), could be read along its "backward trajectory" of power. In this regard, Gramsci's notion of "organic crisis" could be here employed for displaying how historical epoch cannot be dismantled without being subjected to an "already-working movement" of a new entity leading to power by producing a new one (Hall 1987). As a result of a further "power change", which irremediably dismisses and sets apart certain segments of society as a *conditio sine qua non* for letting another one emerge, divide, and rule over, collective identities struggling to come into being found themselves in-between at first. The role of subaltern segments of society is quite interesting to highlight along with the multiplicity of dispersed wills and heterogeneous aims they (wanted, but they failed to) represent. In other words, in time of "organic crisis", they play the role of collective entities which, while in the struggle to emerge and seek out a full degree of public recognition, end up being discarded within a pluralisation of cultural identities. At the same time, attempts to emerge along the lines of uneven historical development shape new forms of political and cultural orders. They represent a "hostile exterior" for the new realm which is about to come. This is why they are instrumentally displaced through a fabrication of externally imposed ascriptions that depict their identities and behaviour patterns as incompatible, threatening, foreign neighbours, harmful communities, disloyal organisations, and so forth.

In the aftermath of the Communist experience, the paradigm of the "organic crisis" is centrally paramount to comprehend the identity building that old-fashioned minority groups (e.g., religious, ethnic or sub-national) and those newly-arrived minorities, (e.g., migrant, LGBTQI+, or even disabled communities) have been externally exposed to. Although their arrival, and the inconspicuous struggle for recognition, began to impinge on post-Communist societies from within, a look beneath the surface of chronology-centred historical events is

---

[3] Madina Tlostanova, cit., Public Lecture "The Post-Colonial Condition, the DeColonial Option and the Post-Socialist Elephant in the Room", Faculty of Political Science, University of Belgrade, for the workshop "Dialoguing 'Between the Posts' Post-socialist and post-/de-colonial perspectives on domination, hierarchy and resistance in South-Eastern Europe", 14 June 2019.

relevant to shed new lights on the trajectory that certain segments of society have been posited along while falling into a marginalised human condition. Paradoxically in the post-1989 era, indeed, those most vulnerable societal groups, particularly ethnic, gender and sexual minorities, which were exposed to change after an epoch of invisibility, became those social categories that had, in theory, the greatest window of opportunity, but, in practice, the greatest losses during that period of time (Ilisei 2017: 57).

On the one hand, as largely explained in the Marxist literature and its scholarship, minority cultures were nothing but hegemonic blocs that missed the chance to emerge and thereby impose themselves, or at least mediate with the counter-bloc, prior to becoming subaltern and culturally marginal in the post-1989 era. As Gramsci pointed out, indeed, the possibility of falling into a subaltern position in the aftermath of the "organic crisis" is made dependent on the ability of the only one limited historical actor that presents its own emancipation as equivalent to the emancipation of the society as a whole. Despite being on the verge of crisis, political forces struggle to conserve and defend the existing structure by making every effort to cure them within certain limits and thereby overcome them. These incessant and persistent efforts [...] upon the terrain of the "conjunctural" display how the forces of opposition organise themselves (1971: 178). Similar to Fanon's post-colonial analysis, the post-Communist limited historical actor is one of the two (or more) hegemonic blocs coming into struggle by unfolding themselves into political and cultural agencies. It is the tribe that makes itself into a party by speaking on behalf, and in praise, of the totality of people (Fanon 2011: 147) – which was the social ethnic majority in the post-1989 CEE. In this struggle of emergence and replacement of the "former" hegemony, only one historical bloc in struggle with others manages to employ its ideological set of ideas and values (e.g., religion, education, media, family roles, and so on). It, therefore, becomes dominant throughout its attempts to strive to secure consent and exclude the other, rather than functioning in the interests of the society as a whole. Thus, by keeping up with the time of crisis, only one historical bloc will be maintaining itself as such (Strinati 1995: 170). In this regard, a new hegemony came to emerge by going to the detriment of the other as well as replacing the former one, imposing a new constitutive ruling majoritarian "ethnos" as an ideological instrument to divide the realm and rule over. Thus, a minority perspective in Communism's organic crisis in CEE suggests to see historical (trans-)/formations of the realm as a process of domestication of those left behind, for example, those sub-national minorities posited in different contexts than the one the previous national minorities occupied in the previous system. In few words, all of these pose the structural basis of the Theory of Hegemony and its implications for the identities. In fact, throughout an organic crisis, hegemonic bloc's struggle for emergence paves the way to the formation of an ideology, which displays a new set of elements and values that guarantee the emerging hegemonic bloc to keep "others" at check and imposing upon them a new "common sense" over which they will politically rule and reign by maintaining a new political order (Checkin 2016: 22–23), namely, a new status quo.

On the other hand, however, none can nowadays claim that such "subaltern groups" have been pauperised from a high degree of recognition or threatened to death. Yet, minority issues distress post-Communist societies and their democracy transition epoch. Among others, almost forgotten breakaway republics as well as "frozen conflicts" in the Caucasus have been recently revitalised from "organic crisis" in Southeast Ukraine and 2014 Annexation of annexation by the Russian Federation; moreover, the EU-facilitated process toward EU accession for Western Balkan countries has paradoxically generated the idea to swap territories between Kosovo and Serbia along majoritarian-ethnic lines. In the Baltic region, ethnic Russians continue to be constantly observed and monitored due to the apparently leading-threat role they (might) play in the society they live in, challenging State sovereignty and principles of post-Soviet statehood; ethnic minority groups in other countries (e.g., ethnic Turks in Bulgaria, Hungarians in Romania, Serb separatists in Bosnia, among others) continue to be stigmatised as a leading-threat for human security on a local level, and territorial integrity and internal stability on a more regional level.

If not yet clarified, it is no longer logical to label a given minority group as a leading-threat per se for the core society. In contrast, a specific debate should be opened, in Spivak's language, about the space of marginalisation. The latter is squarely interlinked with Gramsci's "organic crisis" and the instrumental displacement of one of the two (or more) blocs in struggle for emergence and recognition. Such "displacement", however, does not literally recall an idea of spatial exclusion, ghettoisation, or public ostracism understood as a constriction, delimitation of a social entity's space of existence, or geographical separateness from the "centre" of the wider public. Neither does it simply refer to what Fukuyama addresses as "megalothymia", that is, a kind of individual desire based on personhood's will of being recognised as superior than an "other", whose inferiority does not in turn receive public recognition for their human or collective worth (2018: 21). While social sciences have always stressed the paramount need to fully recognise minority groups into the wider public and accommodate them accordingly, Spivak pointed out that subaltern cultures or collectives do not exclusively need a cultural recognition or political representation. A dismissal of "culture", namely of "knowledge" (e.g. knowledge exploitation), is the real shaper of minority conditionality and marginality. It hence seems clearer than in the past that minority groups know how the outside realm works, how to manage the relationship with the State (e.g., central authority), with the market they go to, with the magical interconnectedness of global forces into the locality they live in, and how to transmit and convey their claims. It is so indeed since their subalternity provides chances to get benefits. Looking underneath the status of marginalisation, the creation of subalternity ascribes a certain identity along with a behaviour pattern, which mirrors identity itself; in addition, such externally imposed ascription of political and cultural subordination, especially among those who are aware of it, comes to represent the only one perspective through which those who are subjected to it, are able to be represented and seek representation for themselves. Subalternity is therefore nothing but the externally imposed shaper of minorityhood understood firstly as a human condition of cultural inferiority and only secondly as a political or spatial dislocation. So far, attempting to challenge the ethnically-defined exclusive bases of political actorness within the contemporary democracies of CEE, has produced struggles for imposing counterarguments against minority status of subalternity (e.g., exclusion, marginalisation, ghettoisation, and so forth). As Laclau pointed out, a State can constitute an instance of topography due to its political inability to identify and fully recognise all its entities from within. It can thus turn out that such instance unleashes a rejection of these entities from the State itself. As the time has passed by, post-Communist public spheres have reproduced such instance of topography since 1989 up until today, legitimising instrumentally certain (hegemonic) entities to the detriment of (subaltern) others.

Following Jürgen Habermas's public sphere model, Gramsci's category of subalternity shows how post-Communist positionality of minority groups manifests itself by unfolding the existence of a large number of, perhaps inconspicuous, yet salient, voices to which the public sphere and its institutions remain deaf. While the existence of one universal, inclusive, and discursive public sphere, within which all members of society have access to, and are freely involved by positing themselves along public's or counterpublic's argumentations[4], Gramsci's

---

[4] Jürgen Habermas's work "The Structural Transformation of the Public Sphere" (published originally in 1960 and translated into English only in 1989) identifies the pillars of the so-called public sphere and its rational instrument for improvement of public affairs.

notion of subalternity might here raise a sub-question related to the accessibility of the public sphere itself. In fact, a Gramscian perspective questions whether or not Habermas's public sphere model entails that everybody's participation in a discursive arena should be in theory free and constantly open to everybody's critical formulation of argumentation and counter-argumentation without being at the same time subject to any power pressure or external domination. In Habermas's sense, subaltern positionality is formally and discursively guaranteed, yet the degree of equal influence that each autonomous member possesses is today's major concern. In this ideal model, Habermas's principle of universal public sphere is based on the implementation of *ratio* (e.g., reason, argument) by which the "private" is defined as opposite to the "public", which is thus the result of a formulation and redefinition of issues within, and in between, the public and the counter-public. Both are aimed at checking-and-balancing the regulatory mechanisms of inclusion and rational discussion of certain issues (e.g., theory of validity claims), which often tend to be discarded or left out, and to oppose the *voluntas* (e.g., will) representing intellectually inert power politics (Vavřík 2010: 105). The "private" is here opposed to the "public". In contrast to such public sphere model, Nancy Fraser criticised the assumption of such "universal" and per se inclusive public sphere (1992), (re-)considering the dual dimension of publics and counter-publics. In venturing the discursive parapet of the counter-publics from within, Fraser mainly pointed out how dual functions of Habermas's public sphere dismiss *counter-publics within a counter-public*, which thereby become subaltern. To put it simply, she unravels the existence of subaltern voices within already-dominated voices that compose counter-publics, ones that tend in turn to be oftentimes dismissed by the confrontational manifestation with the dominant public composed of the dominant public discourse of hegemons. This, which sheds light on how subtly hegemonic functions lead to implicit relations of domination, shows the systematically generated relations of cultural and political relations created in the public discourse, where dominance and subordination are manifest according to imposed power structures. "Subaltern counter-publics-within-a-counter-public" seems perfectly to coincide, and be the representative of, "subaltern minority voices-within-a-minority voice" which is legitimate to have its discursive space. Such juxtaposition is here worth reconsidering in light of the lack of equal participation that results from subaltern voices being dismissed and denied in their struggle to formulate needs, claims, and requests from within the counter-public itself. For example, the newly-arrived minority groups and their crucial voices represent the hidden, the voiceless and unheard from within minority groups, which, in confrontation to the ethno-nationalist hegemonic blocs (e.g., limited historical actor in Gramsci's terminology) continue to be disqualified at the expense of the dominated mainstream that the counter-publics represent. Thus, on the one side, these subaltern minority counter-publics are dismissed by being kept away from "having a say" and from a roughly equal access to the public sphere through the counter-public voice, and are thereby maintained voiceless and/or kept in check within the same counter-public they belong to, on the other side. In this regard, the composition of public and counter-public discourse that Habermas had coherently theorised in the 1960s displays the asymmetry-led instrumental imposition of the historical bloc that Gramsci earlier was capable of understanding and explaining. Although Habermas's public sphere model seems reductive in front of today's growing complexity of power and public realm (Vavřík 2010: 1112), Habermas himself welcomed Fraser's critique. Both have been used as a point of departure for the study of the post-Communist public sphere. However, Gramsci's "organic crisis" provides a different perspective for investigating beyond the dual exclusion of minority groups from the public sphere and the critique of the lack of participatory parity in any public debate.

Gramsci's notion of "subaltern" does not only realise how historical crisis-emerging blocs lead ahead in the attempt to seek power out and secure dominant position by instrumentally displacing others' voices. At the same time, as Gramsci had realised[5], subalternity possesses in itself an internal separation of roles and identities of representation based on a discursive strategy that subaltern actorness possesses in order to confront the dominant (hegemonic) voice. It often follows that absence of internal confrontation between the voices that the counter-public is composed of consequentially leads to the risk of rendering such voices dually subaltern and dominated, by reducing them into a type of "We" that each minority group is ascribed to (e.g., minorityhood), and operating to the disregard of the same minority and to the advantage of the dominant public discourse. For example, it has been historically

---

[5] In Southern Italy, Gramsci's analysis of peasantry and rural areas is extremely important for understanding the societal role of organic and traditional intellectuals in relation to the dominant hegemonic power structure and discourse, in The Continental Philosophy Reader (ed. Kearney and Rainwater), 1996, "The Formation of the Intellectuals", p.192 n.3) Similarly, Gramsci noticed how within "the Kingdom of Yugoslavia, Serbian forces or those favourable to Serb hegemony are the forces which oppose agrarian reforms. Both in Croatia and in the other non-Serb regions we find that there is an anti-Serb rural intellectual bloc, and that the conservative forces are favourable to Serbia. In this case, too, there do not exist local "hegemonic" groups – they are under the hegemony of Serbia; meanwhile the subversive forces do not have, as a social function, any great importance. Anybody who observes Serb affairs superficially might wonder what would have happened if so-called brigandage of the kind which occurred round Naples and in Sicily from 1860 to 1870 had occurred in Yugoslavia after 1919." In A. Gramsci (1971) "Selection of Prison Notebooks".

proven that in the Balkan region the primary victims of exclusion from hegemonic position within the counter-publics have always been the peasantry, regardless of ethnic distinctions, particularly those who dared to raise their heads in a regime of brutal repression and enormous poverty (Chomsky 1999: 50). In this regard, while the dialectical relationship between the two functions of hegemony instrumentally disqualify as "private", "illegitimate", or "irrational" a large number of minority voices from within the counter-public, the latter remain overlooked and unheard, thus subordinate twice (Warner 2002: 84). The examples of LGBTQ communities within Muslim groups, or the critical voices of the "extrovert insiders" among Kosovo Serbs, are instructive.

In other words, these examples are instructive to give credits to what Laclau and Mouffe referred to relation of subordination between an employee with respect to an employer, a certain form of family with another, a woman with respect to man in certain contexts, and so on (1985: 153-154). This relation of subordination is shaped by a purely cultural form of tradition, rite, stereotype, or cliché in their purely repetitive forms of being performed. In addition, following again Laclau and Mouffe, all relations of subordination can potentially affect intra-group dynamics on a political level, and be thereby experienced as relations of oppression on a cultural one (Marchart 2018: 124).

Beyond doubt Gramsci's tandem of hegemony and "organic crisis" continues to remain central for dealing philosophically with subaltern cultures and identities. For instance, following Gramsci's steps of "organic crisis", Checkin (2016: 36) points out that there are periods of historical time where potential change is not particularly challenged. It can last for a long time, and can be very differently resolved: by restoration, by reconstruction, or by passive transformation of cultural and political power structures. Sometimes it can last for decades (Gramsci 1971: 178), sometimes it can be more stable rather than more unstable at other times. However, as Gramsci also noticed, a potential "organic crisis" occurs by marking profoundly the political society, by paving the way to a different direction in life among people (e.g. common sense), by affecting cultural institutions and their actors, and thereby putting the whole realm at stake. For example, minority groups have begun to exclusively rely on their own personal effort as a way of improving their lives; yet, they feel the world they live in cannot be changed. It is "too big and too terrible", or a condition analogous to "from heaven to hell" quoting Wunsch's study on civil society mobilisation in Southeast Europe (2018).

Overall, such scenario does not suggest to propose a change in opposition with those previously emerged conditions which preceded gradually, and largely imperceptibly throughout the "organic crisis". This exceptional duration means that incurable structural contradictions have revealed themselves and, by reaching their maturity, they with difficulty tend toward a definitive (dis-)aster. All of these leave space to confront Gramsci's critique of the industrial societies of the West and issues that post-Communist contemporary democracies struggle with. In particular, the prism of "organic crisis" cannot be only taken into account for tracing back the collapse of the Communist experience. Rather, it can bring to light the time of fixation of those nodal points around which new meanings of the societal, the political, and the cultural performativity emerge all together by imposing themselves at the expense of certain groups whose double-bind identity of political subordination and cultural inferiority is ascribed.

Therefore, Gramsci's "organic crisis" displays here phenomena of "positive discrimination" throughout society, and behind which blatant attempts of the leading hegemonic bloc to secure its power position are made by all means possible in order to impose its indigenous leaderships (Kushnir 2018: 137). Within this, it is possible to deeply understand the reasons for which normative recognition of minority rights, regardless of ethnic, gender, or sub-national feature, remain a concern and at the mercy of majoritarian cultural models and their hegemonic forces. Hence, application of the so-called "organic crisis" of Gramsci over the 1989 breakdown shifts the attention to the general understanding of the category of "post". With a particular reference to the sphere of colonial studies here, the category of the "post" is neither a chronologically determined conclusion of the previous cultural and political system, nor a historical indicator of the beginning of a new epoch.

After the Communist era in CEE, such "post" has been often (mis)understood as the momentum where history began to shift definitively gears towards full-fledged democracy, thereby changing the terrain toward a new moment of history that came finally into being. Through the notion of coloniality understood as a human condition, the category of *post*-Communism cannot be understood as a setting for a horizon of hope. Without discrediting history and its investigation and methodology, post cannot display, and be composed of, a simple chronologically threefold paradigm of "beginning-throughout-after". If we attempt to philosophically establish a dialogue between the post-colonial and the *post*-Communist in order to lay out a different angle of investigation, we are not only dealing with an entirely new conception of crisis and of power. Neither do we only face, as Hall pointed out, a superficial, normal explanation of the structural disruption of the previous economic, social, and cultural order that ceased to provide its own form of domination through language and power (1987). Instead, we may deal with a potential momentum that lasts, as Cheskin (2016) has described, indicating a socio-cultural and political trajectory along which the habits of being remain unaltered. In other words, a structural crisis occurring at various places and times, thereby lasting along pre-emerging moments of definitive (dis-)aster and new emergence of hegemonic blocs, is not hermetically passing by. Throughout, we may be able to discern not only a momentum of definitive (dis-)aster, but also a tracing-back trajectory of historical events whose legacy shows restructuring, refashioning, and reorganisation of the political and cultural structures of society. To put it simply, a legacy along which the same people, who think the same thoughts, whose interests and ways to seek them out remain the same, is still at work. In this regard, a post-colonial angle of philosophical investigation employs nothing but yet another paradigm to look at history not just chronologically, but along its historical passages.

According to the subject-matter of this study, we might be capable once again of using the category of coloniality in the *post*-Communist societies, not as a theoretical notion for setting up a liberation struggle in accordance with what orthodox Marxism may suggest. Rather, it might be used for displaying how the coexistence of ethnic-majoritarian assumptions with the aspiration of "normal European democracy" (Dawson 2016) came to be established, thereby navigating in between a hegemonic bloc's formation into pre-emergence time and space and its imposition through a discredit of an "other". In this sense, we might thus be able to trace the formally colonial-type form of possession of knowledge among subaltern groups, whose work continues—despite all potential recognition of minority claims and cultures—to negate, disavow, distort, and deny access to different forms of certain knowledge and the life vision represented by different subjectivities. This is, at the very end, the main reason why old and newly arrived minority groups continue to remain subaltern, experiencing a feeling of non-existence despite the fact that legal recognition has been partially or fully achieved. Hence, a proper question to raise is whether the post-Communist "organic crisis" is over, thus definitively turned into a closed subject of scholarly enquiry, or it is still at work. A partial response to such question, perhaps satisfactory enough, has been given in the past few decades by scholars and academics.

Svetlana Alexievich, Belarusian oral historian, argues that "Socialism is over, but we are still there"; Madina Tlostanova, most well-known for her post-colonial feminist account, pays attention to the so-called "post-

Socialist elephant in the room"[6]; the philosopher Boris Groys, too, touches upon the issues of a post-Communism performed and lived backwards, a movement against the flow of time through which its subject has set sail not from the past toward the future, but from the wished future toward the past.

For example, a continuity of a historically imposed subordination of the Turkish minority in Bulgaria persisted throughout Communist and post-Communist élites transformation. In fact, the Bulgarian Socialist Party (BSP), main heir of the political culture of the previous Communist regime, managed to keep ethnic Bulgarians mobilised against the restoration of cultural rights of the Turkish minority in the same way Communist rulers did, forcing all "Communist Turks of Bulgaria" to align themselves with a Slavic identification. This paved the way to the enigmatic position of Bulgaria's de facto "ethnic minority party". While the minority group managed to seek out recognition in 1991 and secured its political representation through the Turkish-nominated Movement for Rights and Freedoms (MRF), which succeeded to uphold basic cultural rights for Bulgaria's ethnic Turks, yet such recognition did not occur "on ethnic basis".

On the contrary, a more hybrid legitimisation of liberal values, particularly necessary for the post-Communist Bulgaria, shed light on a historical trajectory which continues nowadays to deter political expression of nonBulgarian identities rather than Bulgarian nationalism (Rechel 2007), affecting today's position of the MRF organisation on the ground. While deterioration of public opinion of Islam and Bulgarian Muslims has accelerated and referred to a form of banal nationalism (Billig 1995) and recollection of a period of Bulgarian history, the MRF represents an "enigma-within-an-enigma" (Leview-Sawyer 2015). While it seems to be culturally paramount for Bulgarian élites to offer anti-Turkish rhetoric and be seen to shun political cohabitation with the MRF, the latter has taken part in different majority coalitions in the Parliament in the last years to keep close and unhealthy relations with economic élites (Pedersen and Johannsen 2011: 89). While Bulgaria's majoritarian cultural system accuses the MRF of stoking ethnic tensions across the country (Dawson 2014: 163), the MRF counteracts by claiming itself as the sole peacemaker and guarantor of ethnic peace. Despite the constitutional ban for all political entities against the use of ethnic basis for constituting political organisations, MRF plays the role of standard-bearer among Muslim Romani as well as Turks and other small, hybrid

---

[6] *Ibidem*, Madina Tlostanova. in her public lecture "The Post-Colonial Condition, the De-Colonial Option and the Post-Socialist Elephant in the Room".

groups, such as the Bulgarian Pomaks. To sum up, while the post-Communist "organic crisis" has maintained the Bulgarian ruling ethnos in power and its dominant structures, the subaltern Turkish entity has only had the opportunity to enjoy hegemonic structures. Among others, it is self-explanatory how the MRF formed a coalition with the Bulgarian Socialist Party (2013–2014), the social entity which forbade at first their recognition in the post-1989 era.

In the same vein, the worsening conflict in Nagorno-Karabakh, that is, the oldest and longest military confrontation between two post-Soviet Republics, has impinged on Armenia and Azerbaijan's population. Ruling élites have constantly manipulated collective memories in both countries, thereby conveying to the youngest generations of Armenians and Azerbaijanis narratives of what *really* happened that taboo any sort of pacification. As a result, a "culture of peace" seems impossible to win the ground in the public spheres, leading Armenians toward a phenomenon of so-called "trap of national unity" (Zhamakochyan 2017). Constantly devoted to de-humanising the Other (Ayunts, Zolyan, and Zakaryan 2016), continuously manipulated exacerbation of both perception and projections of the conflict narrative is given back to the public consciousness, into the public sphere and wider discourse, public schools and higher education curricula, public broadcasting, academic publication, and so forth. Although historical memory is instrumentally constructed in order to correspond with favourable events, which omit facts and neglect contexts with the purpose of justifying national narratives (Harris 2012), post-Soviet Armenian citizenry's tendency to elect politicians belonging to the so-called "Karabakh Clan" (Kirvelyté 2015: 29) is self-explanatory[7]. On the other side, the Azerbaijani scenario displays at least a political pluralism that, despite its low level, seems to be different from the neighbouring Azerbaijan the Aliev dynasty began to rule in 1993. Alike Armenia's political belongingness tied with Karabakh, the former President Hydar Aliev (1993–2003) and his son Ilham Aliev, currently ruling as President of the young Republic, belong to de jure exclave of Nackichevan, landlocked and bounded by Armenia and Iran with a short border with Turkey, which continues to suffer from its geographic position and the conflict with Armenia.

All of these open up yet another perspective with regards to today's minority issues. While the rise of States and constitution of their new

---

[7] Following Ter-Petrosyan, who had no personal ties with Nagorno-Karabakh, both last two Presidents of Armenia, Robert Kocharyan, who was previously president of de facto Nagorno-Karabakh Republic (1994–1997) and Prime Minister of Armenia (1997–1998), as well as the current Armenian President Serzh Sarkisyan (2008– current mandate), who is the second de facto head of Karabakh Armed Forces, come originally from the disputed region.

public spheres constituted, in Gramsci's words, a new ethical-political momentum of society, the Communist "organic crisis" opened up the impossibility of a few cases to identify entities in the public sphere since the State itself constituted an instance within a topography (Laclau 2000: 50). As mentioned above in accordance with the issue of subaltern counter-publics, Fraser argues that the latter have constituted parallel discursive arenas where members of subordinate groups are keen to circulate counter-discourse in order to formulate oppositional, and confrontational, interpretations of their identities, interests, and needs (1992: 122). In this way, the growth of parallel communities began to be discussed more widely and the concept of (post)multiculturalism began to come in from a critical perspective (Murray 2018: 102; see conclusions). Without any doubt, for example, the constitution of parallel counter-publics within minority groups came into being through the collapse of the Communist regime and during the nation-building process of states with historically contested territories. By following Gramsci's language, the "1989 organic crisis" meant nothing but the demise of a complex identity project composed of a multiplicity of countries, religions, and classes that from a Nation-style togetherness ended up being scattered across a region to reinvent, or, more properly, to reimagine. From this perspective, post-1989 passage to action of CEE towards freedom and democracy (Gržinić 2000: 69) could be understood as a failure to have succeeded in inscribing the entire region on the map of political, cultural, or artistic events in Europe. As a matter of fact, the region could no longer be understood as a geographical "ground zero", a "buffer zone" between the West and the East, an interactive area between inclusion/exclusion as well as universalism/localism.

Hence, if we would here argue that Gramsci's "organic crisis" is still lasting after having manifested itself since 1989, we would, therefore, confront the issue of post-Communist subaltern positionality. It is instructive indeed that vibrant return of imagined sovereignty of communities continues to revitalise regional obsession for spatial re-appropriation of historically contested lands of origins, which were defined as pacified (e.g., 2014 Crimea annexation, Serbian breakaway entity in Bosnia), or on the road to complete stabilisation (e.g., Kosovo/Serbia proposal for territorial swap along ethno-majoritarian lines), or which have recently gone through new chapters of militarily escalated disputes and contestations after being (arguably) defined as "frozen conflicts" (e.g., Armenia-Azerbaijan conflict, Moldova and pro-Russia de facto entity, Romania's Hungarian-majority areas).

While Slavoj Žižek has argued that the reality of the region could be based on the utopian idea summarised by the word "Bosnia", in which the direct consequence of today's (continuous) backlashes is nothing but the result of having submitted a State to the power struggles of ethnic communities, what is really weakening us, and missing in the word "Bosnia", is not a unified State authority elevated above ethnic disputes (Žižek 1993) but a lack of ontologically empirical investigation of minority "everyday life" in "their" psychical experience, and "their" cultural everyday language. Rural and isolated, or urban and more vibrant, in all post-Communist States the issue of the public sphere has always recalled that of "space" in terms of minority positionality and, above all, marginality. For example, the case study of Roma Muslims represents not only an issue-within-anissue, but it traditionally touches upon the issue of self-marginalisation of "ungoverned communities" whose long history of nomadism and exteriority to the State's cultural system creates a high level of uncontrolled mobility, unfair taxation, and so forth.

By keeping a constant reference to Gramsci's "organic crisis", while it seems lasting due to its mature stage of manifestation across the region, a post-colonial perspective might help to touch upon issues of such spatialisation. A lot has been written about it. However, a minority perspective over such subject matter might here be useful to re-examine the historically power-related modalities of how post-Communist Europe was rapidly truncated from within by a wealth of struggles for the re-appropriation of historical lands of origin, e.g. spaces of belonging. Having gained a scholarly popularity in the so-called "politics of space", never-ending contestation over the issues of super-national dependency on neighbourly (kin-)states, contested territorial integrity, and allocation of self-governing rights (e.g., regional autonomy) are inflaming the wider public and dangerously putting at risk newly-affirmed principles of sovereignty of the new States. In parallel, the constant search for definitive taxonomies for defining "peoplehood", particularly regarding minority groups, juxtaposes the return of "imagined sovereignties" (Olson 1996:108) whose ideas of collective subject and normative forces became immediately one of the key dilemmas. After being remapped in the aftermath of the Second World War and brutally included in the socialist world, the post-1989 order reduced CEE to a typical product of Western modernity looking at its non-absolute other form from outside and, consequently, homogenising its multiplicity and diversity following the well-known logic of either neglecting the other or misinterpreting it as the same or as the predecessor of the same (Tlostanova 2008:1).

The controversial category of post-Communist (colonial) human condition of subaltern cultures and groups shifts gears onto a different, perhaps more abstract, terrain of investigation. To a large extent, postCommunist minority positionality is no longer entirely dominated by space, but by categories of time, as in the preceding period of high modernism proper, as Spivak had pointed out (1999:313). In this regard, there is no longer an authentic position from which to speak and to represent oneself, one that normative approaches and disciplines have tried to identify in order to empower people. On the contrary, minority positionality and its subaltern conditionality deal first and foremost with(in) a complicated social and historical context which, in turn, have come to assign, shape, and constitute collective identities. Application of Gramsci's "organic crisis" touches upon a different kind of societal positionality externally imposed by taking distance, interestingly enough, from the Marxist approach of pre-existing "structures" that have an impact on minority (subaltern) scope for improving their conditions (Schwandner-Sievers 2019: 22). In time of the overwhelmingly employed identity politics, "who an individual is" as well as "where this individual comes from" (Taylor 2010: 54) do not only play an awakening role among collective entities. In contrast, "where are we, now?" has been partially replaced by a "where are you *really* from?" which implies an existential space designating routes of pleasure and desire, judgements, and dreams (Henry 2003). This is what one should consider as a space of subaltern marginality.

As previously stated, such space of marginality does not reflect a spatial exclusion understood as an article of geography. It is the result of power fabrication that culturally frames and shapes a certain human condition. As Timothy Luke argued, space does not exist as such; it too must be fabricated continuously by the production and reproduction of society (1996: 120, mentioned by Oliver Marchart 2018: 95). It thus results from the mechanical making and re-making of the operational functions of institutions, which continuously push "out of space" by dislocating – namely, setting apart, a certain segment of society and its culture.

From a minority perspective in the post-Communist region, such marginal positionality cannot only concern issues of resurgence and revival of regionalisms and ethno-nationalisms aiming at constructing space in accordance with people's biological imprint, birth circumstances, intellectual properties, or moral sensibility. In this regard, the space-and-identity dichotomy does not have only territorial, geographical, or physical boundaries. While in the Communist time, particularly within the Soviet Union, the concept of the border was an impenetrable barrier, impregnable and liable to sudden change, contemporary reference to maps has become definitely more mental and psychological rather than real, where boundary delineation relates to more abstract space and diverse concepts of boundaries (Zambelli 2008).

Space has thus become more than a physical terrain of contestation. Hence, a minority perspective is useful to venture such notion of space as a physical terrain of contestation understood through the dichotomies of centre-versus-periphery, centralisation-versus-federalisation, and so forth. In doing so, this approach toward the space tends to refuse, a certain relational theory which portrays the former Eastern bloc as the "unconscious Orient" where phenomena of ethnic separatism, violence and turbulences have a spatial confrontation (Hale 2008: 33). It unravels a human condition instead, one of marginal essence which began to show how the location in the realm has been fixated in terms of positive (positivist?) terms of the actual historical geography of contingency (Rajan 1993: 9). Perhaps this is why even the EU-facilitated process of stabilisation of Kosovo-Serbia relations, aimed at driving both countries' EU accession, has produced the idea of Kosovo's partition for pacifying the territorial rivalry. If one would read the recent history of Kosovo's statehood and its related issues with the formerly Serbled hegemonic system during the Yugoslavian time, one would see how such a proposal of "territorial swap" is not new at all. It was between 1992 and 1993, in fact, when the President of Yugoslavia, Dobrica Ćosić, proposed in discreet contacts with Kosovo Albanian leadership to partition Kosovo's territory along ethno-majoritarian lines, thereby separating Serb enclaves from the rest of the Albanian-populated areas. Yet more surprisingly, rejection of such proposal in protection of Kosovo's historical territorial integrity was announced in 1993 and 2018 alike. Whether the question raising the issue of hegemonic culture-oriented understating of Kosovo as a "Serbian colony" would go too far, a post-colonial perspective over this specific microregional dispute shows interesting facets. If we consider Gramsci's "organic crisis" as a lasting period of time throughout which historical blocs tend to emerge (e.g. the power bloc, the elite, "la casta"), today's legal-political failure and diplomatic ineptitude of élites in Kosovo is just instructive. In insights, a post- colonial paradigm over the (hegemonic and) cultural sense of Serbian superiority towards Kosovo's Albanians is rendered visible by the Serbian narrative of the Battle of Kosovo Polje (1389), which proudly recollects the desperate attempt of Christian Serbian soliders to halt the onrushing armies of the malignant and majestic corrupt Ottomans (Winchester 1999). The vernacular speech gave by the Serb Prime Minister, Ana Brnabić, Serbian lesbian political figure, who recently referred to Kosovo's Albanians as people belonging to the jungle, is a self-explanatory of such narrative.

Similarly, from a majority perspective, a comparison between "spatial proximity" and "marginality" does not follow common lines. In Central

Bulgaria, the decision of the Local Council of Stara Zagora to "Bulgarize" place-names with a clearly Turkish or Arabic origin has opened yet another chapter of an endless debate in the post-Communist history of Bulgaria. Similar proposals for name-changing in other municipalities demonstrate how a perceived rather than an actual threat coming from the Turkish minority is continuously represented. Paradoxically, but unsurprisingly, the name-change regulation voted by the Local Council of Stara Zagora happened during the Bulgarian Presidency of the Council of the EU; just a few weeks later at the Sofia Summit, Bulgaria called for an implementation of the EU integration plans for the Western Balkan countries whose Muslim and Turkish heritage is part of their national identity, such as in Bosnia and North Macedonia.

To partially conclude, here marginalisation of cultures or communities remains related to the issue of post-Communist positionality because it is constantly written in the history of power, as Foucault might point out (1980:149). Today's minority contestations of "space" are reduced to no more than symbolic, and politics-oriented, discursive strategies by authorities to serve their short-term interests related to gains at polls, instruments of control and constant association of new narrative through constructions of exclusive discourse rather than specific physical objects (e.g., statues, religious spaces, checkpoints). Therefore, a perspective *from below* highlights how politics of space has left room for a serious question over issues related to politics of location. In other words, a socio-political as well as philosophical enquiry to address through voices spoken from where they are, rather than about where they are from.

Once again, according to the subaltern positionality into the public sphere, which is a direct spatial reference throughout civil society, structures of (instrumental) exclusion remain stably as such in order to come into being and therefore exist. From a minority position, structures of exclusion do not only show the dialectical nature of hegemony and the nature of its establishment. It also displays how one of the two poles of its structure (State/civil society) performs itself by denying the potential reversal of the dialectic's power. This is why Gramsci juxtaposes civil society, namely – a powerful system of fortresses and earthworks (Gramsci 1971:238), to the State (see Laclau 2000:48). All of these might cause a completely philosophical turmoil over the discourse among those who govern and upon those who are governed, yet a turning-point which could pave the way towards an unrest of the tradition of power (e.g., Carl Schmitt) and tradition of oppressed (e.g., Walter Benjamin). However, so far, in CEE, subaltern counter-publics can be identified through the asymmetric lines that the post1989 "organic crisis" is still maintaining itself as such, thereby constructing a discourse to keep knowledge in check, reflecting it upon segments of society, and instrumentally posited into the wider public.

CHAPTER SIX
"(Re-)thinking Subalternity and the Necessity of Hegemony

Similar to the notion of "organic crisis", the Theory of Hegemony is without any doubt the central pillar of Gramsci's contribution to Continental philosophy in general, and Marxology in particular. Moreover, such Gramscian philosophical category has played a pivotal role in the development of the interdisciplinary approach in the field of social sciences. In addition, the legacy of Gramsci's category of hegemony has not only been of great help for re-politicising the sphere of everyday life and culture, but concomitantly for occluding a political function of hegemony (McRobbie 1994:51 mentioned by Marchart 2018:119).

Yet, if we should philosophically confront whether or not the postCommunist era has brought its own legacy of power throughout contemporary societies in CEE, we should avoid considering Gramsci's analysis over hegemony in terms of "domination". The word hegemony is ambiguous in English: it has, on the one hand, the meaning of "control" by someone/something over another one, and, on the other hand, in the Marxist literature, it implicates a struggle against "controlling forces". Only a few scholars and academics are worth mentioning while dealing with a coherent understanding of Gramsci's category of hegemony. Among others (e.g., Ernesto Laclau, Chantal Mouffe, Narek Mkrtchyan, Smbat Hovnannisyan), Nataša Kovačević borrows (2008:11-20) a similar approach of the Italian philosopher. She indeed identifies a "hard", mainly political, version of domination whose function is explicitly "imperialist", whose conditions are required by supra-national bodies. In parallel, a "softer" version of domination, mainly cultural, whose colonial function is manifest through ascription of certain "oriental" meanings upon a certain group in society. In few words, only those who consider "hegemony" as a useful category for describing hierarchic imposition and further political disposition, instead of those who follow old-fashioned Marxist proposals of non-mediated action against it, reducing the social realm to the "dominant versus subaltern" paradigm, are worth being mentioned. They understand the teleological potential of Gramsci's hegemony, which can be simply understood as a perspective of opportunities (Hovnannisyan 2016:110). If in the ruling class's hands lies the power of framing and shaping selfhood, there is by default power of counter-framing and counter-shaping among those who are excluded. In this regard, a political ontology of negativity, which would be based on the negation of hegemonic structures and methods of doing politics, would begin with a mediation that, in turn, would inevitably start and be organised into a space of subordination that hegemony vertically imposed. This is, in the very end, the pre-condition to emerge. This would, therefore, become the very holistic condition of emancipation for a whole society and not only for a limited historical actor of the society itself (Laclau 2000:46).

From the perspective of subaltern cultures and groups, we might here avoid the redundant argumentation about whether minority cultures represent a serious threat for our society since "multiculturalism" has gone too far, or, by default, how the above-mentioned post-colonial category of subaltern existence of post-Communist subjects continues to be subjected to political and cultural hegemony.

Gramsci's hegemony — understood in terms of leadership — functions on a political and cultural level through two mutually distinct forces that overlap at the same time. For Gramsci, power does not develop in a given state apparatus, such as in the Parliament or other institutions, nor in a restricted place of society. It is simply distributed by a non-perceivable force throughout society. On the one side, political hegemony relates to the material power of the ruling élites, whose capability of maintaining control is legitimised through use of coercive measures which came into being by instrumentally displacing others. On the parallel side, cultural hegemony is a much subtler and implicit form of control, which does not rest on material force, but influences the realm of ideology. In fact, while cultural hegemony exercises itself through a culture centred domination composed of a system of moral norms and values within a certain societal form of intellectual leadership (Gramsci 1971: 57), political hegemony itself has to be formed by both intellectual and moral unity, which thus creates the fundamental social group dominant over a series of subordinate groups (Gramsci 1971: 181,182). Together, hegemonic functionality passes by material power of the ruling élites that are thus capable of maintaining control through the use of coercive forces and imposition of a unison of economic and political structures.

Hence, while Gramsci's political form of hegemony has been particularly revisited in the Marxist literature as a form of domination to resist and revolt against, the one related to cultural hegemony manifests itself and allows a certain performativity through the imposition of moral and ethical discourse. Its meanings and modalities are vertically imposed upon certain segments of society, whose subalternity also results from imposition of behaviour patterns masked as "common sense". It should be here clear that the mechanism of power domination is not only concentrated in state institutions or in the hands of what could be mistakenly referred to as a political form of authoritative hegemony. Power is, according to Gramsci, concentrated in its form of culture, knowledge, or language, *under-* and *by-which* people give meanings to the outside world, and attribute meanings to things and events (Bayadayn 2015). Because of this, subalternity would eventually lead those who are subjected to forms of discrimination and racism, whose vernacular as well as racist and exclusive form of discourse and performativity exist because legitimised, and, in a few cases, interiorised by those who are affected by.

Many have so far focussed on the operation of how hegemonic forces function through their political and cultural forms of domination; how the latter performs by mutually imposing hierarchical constitutions of power structures in between those who govern, rule over and divide, and those who are governed. Gramsci's Theory of Hegemony has been used methodologically in the circle of social sciences as a fascinating research strategy, one of pedagogical essence, the aim of which is first and foremost to let critical analyses navigate better between multi-layered, differently lodged and epistemologically controverted societal phenomena related to an economic, political, cultural, sociological, or historical perspective. A certain top-down approach of the study of Gramsci's category of hegemony remains undoubtedly central to investigate how hegemonic cultural and political operations of domination are stably at work over society. However, hegemony is even more useful to employ from within those the hierarchic structures hegemony itself is composed of, thereby unravelling the ideological set of values, ideas, knowledge, and performativity ascribed upon so-called subaltern groups. In particular, such "perspective from below" of "Gramscianism" (Mkrtchyan 2016: 109) poses not only the question related to existential process of a given sub-national community, but it does so also by shedding light on ways of conscious internalisation of the model of hegemony by subaltern groups. If hegemony shapes collective social behaviour, the latter is under the influence of a vertically ascribed recognition. Perhaps most importantly, such internalisation of hegemonic subordination renders here hegemony itself a much more useful philosophical category aimed at deepening potential (lack of) recognition of minority groups and their cultural claims. Underneath the parapet of the so-called "hierarchic equality", which is nothing more than one of the major concerns regarding minority cultural rights, ruling hegemony dismisses inter-societal engagements between cultures and restricts their chances to be performed or spoken about (Stepanyan 2016: 84). This is exactly what Gramsci referred to: a subtler leadership on a political and cultural level which operates within a terrain where power structures and ascribed societal identities forcibly channel a specific group to perform and behave accordingly.

Once again here, among a large number of scholars and academics, Gramsci's philosophy as a whole is here considered vital to deepen the basis of specific-group dynamics and their societal controversies and implications. Following the paradigm of hegemony's asymmetrical functionality, the latter manifests itself throughout the society firstly as "domination", bound up with the opposition of State/civil society, and secondly as "hegemonic" *strictu sensu*, in which one historical group secures its dominant leadership over time. Moreover, Gramsci's category of hegemony has an epistemological significance in the social realm. The fact that certain wills of cultural and political autonomy were reborn but abolished through an incorporation within the State activity shows how a wealth of minority demands have been recognised and accommodated only within a certain type of recognition and conditions. Although it might be considered a positive aspect since minority groups have shown lack of advocacy skills in policy-making and reliability in terms of mutual understanding, this opens up a perspective on subaltern identity. According to Gramsci, identity and ideology are almost synonymous in sociality. Precisely, identity manifests itself into a space of influence (e.g., space of existence) which is in turn the space of ideology. Identity is not merely ideology but rather completely influenced by ideology (De Lillo mentioned by Glavanakova 2016) since it results directly from ideological (trans-)formation and (re-)construction of the societal realm (Laclau 1985, Cheskin 2016). It follows that power structures leading the realm by creating hegemonies and enforcing their meanings (Karim and Anjum 2016:39), come to fixate nodal points around which poles of political and cultural dominations are imposed. Under such circumstances, it would no longer be possible for certain groups to escape from being (positively) discriminated (Laclau and Mouffe 1985) or considered equally different. In this instance, it is of extreme importance that those groups who came out from the demise of the Communist experience had come to being, namely to exist, by displacing necessarily an "other" group with whom they were in struggle. Hegemony is not a formation which incorporates everyone indeed (Hall

1987). It has never been, and it will never be. As above pointed out, it is centrally paramount to focus not only on this specified political aspect, but also on the cultural (hegemonic) one.

Focussing on a bottom-up approach, hegemony displays all its subtle and implicit forms of domination. Both political and cultural hegemonic forces render voiceless and powerless those who are considered exempted from a status of subordination, on the majority of whom is conferred a form of recognition and societal representation within certain conditions. Such treatment of recognition of conferment of a societal identity is directly related to hegemonic representation (Quijano 2000:536). As Gramsci had primarily noticed, it is without any doubt a subtler form of ideological domination as it manifests itself in two ways: as domination and moral form of leadership (Gramsci 1971:208). Lack of recognition follows the subtle character of hegemony, which recognises only by following the binarism of two confrontational poles of domination and subordination, rulers and governed, dominant and dominated, and so forth.

Among others, one of the most useful perspectives to deeply understand the subtle mechanism of political and cultural hegemony in the post-Communist societies could refer to today's popular motto of "We, the People". In Butler's language, we may raise the following question: "What kind of 'We' (2016:49–65) came out from the Communist 'organic crisis'?" The Slovak case is here informative. In judicial manners, the preamble of the Slovak constitution is authored not by a kind of 'We' understood in terms 'We, Citizens of Slovak Republic', but by a 'We, Slovak People'" (Elster 1994). Although lawmakers did not have discriminatory purposes against ethnic minority groups, yet they were members of that limited historical bloc which managed to emerge politically and impose themselves culturally throughout the Communist (dis-)aster. Because of this, they did purposely impose a discriminatory legal framework along old-fashioned lines of ethnonational paradigms. They did so because members of that limited historical hegemonic bloc, one that is referred to as the majoritarian cultural system (Kymlicka 1995). For example, in the Bulgarian constitutional text, Article 11 stipulates that "there shall be no political parties on ethnic, racial or religious lines" and Article 36 obliges all Bulgarian citizens to learn the official language. In this regard, despite the fact that "citizens whose mother tongue is not Bulgarian shall have the right to study and use their own language alongside the compulsory study of the Bulgarian language", Art. 36, (2), a language minority policy has never been developed in the country. A legal statement was adopted in accordance with the court decision denying the MRF its original name, "Movement for Rights and Freedoms of the Turks and Muslims in Bulgaria". Immediate pressure on the Council of Europe to push the Bulgarian Constitutional Court to allow the MRF to participate in elections to the Constitutional Assembly of June 10, 1990, was not adequate to bring the MRF back to the original name, which has since then remained "Movement for Rights and Freedoms" without any reference to "Turks" or "Muslims". Similar to other national constitutions of post-Communist CEE, the former Communist idea of "We, the People", which the current Constitution of the Republic of Bulgaria proudly recognises in its preamble, has always been problematic for a complete integration of members belonging to minority groups and newcomers (e.g., refugees, economic migrants, asylum seekers) in the post-1989 era.

Both cases are far different from one of the latest of Croatia's campaigns of support for minority rights and community, in which the Croatian civil society managed to mobilise ethnic Serbs and LGBTQIs by referring to a "We" in terms of "People of Croatia" and not "We, Croats". In fact, the different discursive strategy was constructed around the slogan "Svi mi—za Hrvatsku Svih Nas"—which literally means "All of Us—for Croatia for All of Us" (Wunsch 2018:62).

Therefore, in order to give a response to Butler's question in more philosophical terms, Badiou may prove useful here. The French philosopher has recently noticed how a "We" of this kind is preceded by a "national adjective + people", which refers to a political energy that was dissipated in State formation but that gave to the "official" people the authority to rule over and come to power (2016:109). Paraphrasing Badiou here, post-Communist hegemonic forces came to impose themselves culturally and politically, representing the "official people" around ethno-national lines and instrumentally excluding and marginalising others. Here, it was not an issue to emerge and be supportive around national identities and their majoritarian cultural models. Rather, the main concern did not only regard how newly arrived hegemony affirmed itself by a typically colonialized, exclusive, narrowing, ethnic based, and often aggressive paradigm, but also what really happened to see such violent affirmation of ethno-majoritarian cultural systems. In fact, although they were obliged to protect marginalised, excluded, and subaltern minorities for gaining credibility into an international level, minorities themselves paradoxically fell again into a newly officialised, and legitimized, status of subordination. Instead of achieving their goals via deliberation and consensus, minority groups have started to prefer to trade among themselves through the same notions of ethnicity, religion, sexuality and so on, in other to achieve the achievable. Under such circumstances, they have managed not only to acquire a certain status of recognition, but also secure access to state power and partially benefit from it. To a great extent, as GM Tamás has always argued, one of the reasons of such mistreatment toward minority groups was given by the fact that former Communist party members kept their power position or managed to recycle themselves as new figures and leaders of the façade democracy. Especially in the provinces, in local councils, the police, the economic life, the chambers of commerce, and the post-Communist bourgeois parties, almost nothing really changed (2009:30-35).

First, according to the post-colonial paradigm, it would seem that cultural hegemony patronises certain groups and social perception of them. Second, according to classist Marxist interpretation, those who are subjected to any domination can scarcely perceive and barely understand it. In CEE, instead subalternity shows how particular minority identities are carried out consciously; they are already internalised by those people to whom they have been ascribed, turning them into a form of conscious self-exclusion from political participation and cultural appreciation. Here, the latter could be also understood in terms of ideology. However, the peculiar issue at stake is not what Badiou criticises by comparing subalternity in opposition of being politically engaged. It is not, of course. However, without dismissing such point of view, it is more likely that minority groups have been then only recognised in relation to the new hegemonic majoritarian cultural system, which came to further marginalise them. Some would raise the issue of externally imposed ascriptions that hegemonic forces assign to subaltern groups; others would conversely point out the socio-anthropological aspect of subaltern performativity that has historically investigated how certain communities posit themselves on the margins of society they live in. In between, the real concern of contemporary subaltern groups and communities is that they do not represent anymore a large number of actors of "resistance". While in the current (post-)Marxist and libertarian critical theory, such as in Toni Negri's multitude, there is a renewed interest in localism as well as daily-basis, spontaneous, and immanent form of resistance, which results from a radical interpretation of a reaction against the global Empire and State domination, any subaltern group's political action—a strike, a speech, an assertion of right—shows a parodic component given by a fixated, already institutionalised, practice. The latter results from a logic of constitution, here-and-now performativity of subaltern condition, which is enjoyed and carried out. It follows that what is striking is not what (post)Marxist thinkers continue to consider "resistance" as a sign of subaltern people's agency; rather subalterns themselves make of such position a political strategy, considering it the only way for peoples to change world society in the time of globalisation. Current status of minority groups in post-Communist societies results from inclusion of elements of the hegemonic group by subaltern groups, which thereby undergo some form of hegemony.

Confrontation between hegemonic blocs in struggle to emerge and impose themselves as dominant renders porous hegemonic blocs, opening the doors to minority groups to compromise their subaltern positionality. For example, in post-Communist countries where russification has left marks on political and cultural levels, Alena V. Ledeneva pointed out how the overwhelmingly protean nature of Russian identity, which is labelled as "bunker identity", was put, and perhaps still is nowadays, to work through implementation of a "Sistema" (in Russian: Система), that is, "system". Close to what Gramsci had noticed, Ledeneva pointed out that those living within the Sistema are doomed to either live accordingly or adapt their competencies and liberties into fairly limited circumstances (e.g., restriction of autonomy in Gramsci's language). Those who do so, in fact, manage to update themselves to the Sistema itself, and are doomed later. Those who either cannot or do not want to, are excluded, marginalised, and even forced to emigrate. Interestingly enough, even an "exist option" will thereby have an impact on those who do so (Ledeva 2013: 278, mentioned by Kushnir 2018: 15), imposing a type of negative reflection towards those who did not succeed to enter the Sistema.

Granted, while inclusion of hegemonic elements by subaltern groups is performed in order to exercise, or tend to exercise, hegemony through the mediation of the dominant blocs—the "party" in Gramsci's language—this undoubtedly restricts the field of tropoi which could be dialectically used and employed for contrasting hegemonic forces they are under the effects of. Reconstructing a new form of social identity (Laclau 2000: 78) whose positionality would further move out from the circle of an externally imposed, and internally accepted, subordination, recognition of minority groups would result in hybridity or idiosyncrasy in its form of in-between-ness. However, for Gramsci, the "party" represents not only the hegemonic power structures to struggle against, but also – by the teleological essence of hegemony itself - the "modern Prince". In other words, following the Italian tradition of the Machiavellian Prince (Marchart 2018: 141), the "party" is the potential unifier, a proclaimer and an organiser of an intellectual and moral reform of a society yet to come, raising itself *from below* – namely, from its subaltern conditionality, aiming to create a terrain for the development of a national collective will toward the creation of a superior, total form of modern civilisation (Gramsci 1971: 133). The party, which for Gramsci was beyond doubt the Communist Party of Italy, whose attempt was that of organising the unification of organic workers (e.g. working class) and traditional workers (e.g. peasantry), should be the direct expression of the masses – namely, the energetic spokesperson and the incorruptible defender of the masses (Fanon 2011: 151)

As a matter of fact, there is here yet another interesting convergence on that with many anthropologists studying these issues mentioned above. For instance, it would seem that subaltern groups have stopped including elements of hegemonic domination in order to get something out of it. In the case they might have ceased to do so, such "resistance" takes the forms of a colonised collective action along awakening forces that arise from within an already-imposed space of subordination that those who are subjected to, continue to regard as a space of existence. To put it simply, subaltern groups have culturally interiorised the "inferior position" they have been ascribed, accepting passively their subordination. Thanks to it, they can paradoxically benefit from it. All of these finds best explanation in Gramsci's idea of "spontaneous consent" (Strinati 1995: 165) or "consensual control", whereby individuals "voluntarily" assimilate the worldview or hegemony of the dominant group (Ransome 1992: 150). In turn, subaltern practices of performing as members of a minority group are made instrumentally acceptable.

Because of this, particularly similar to the notion of "organic crisis", hegemony cannot be simply understood only through the opportunity for subalterns of a "liberation struggle" to organise by the use of violence. Hegemonic conditions, which are never a stable entity (Laclau 2000: 150), own the potential to trigger a mobilising and awakening process against the cosiness of the status quo and mediate for a yet another space of existence where subaltern community members may find a way to develop their own knowledge and cultural hegemony. Therefore, perhaps paradoxically, hegemony displays a twofold opportunity.

First and foremost, hegemony is a useful category for condemning externally imposed ascription of subaltern status upon a certain segment of society; second, it is aimed at seeking out full recognition among those who are not yet fully recognised. In other words, as anticipated above, the category of hegemony could be seen simply as a "perspective of opportunities" through which achieving reparation (Mkrtchyan 2016: 110) rather than a violent action of non-mediated liberation could be seen as the goal. This dual angle of investigation makes Gramsci's insight unique and philosophically different from the tradition of orthodox Marxism and Critical Theory's scholars from the Frankfurt School. The latter has historically pointed out the need for an emancipatory discourse of awakening throughout a constitutive momentum that anticipates actions for radical struggle of liberation to be achieved through a full, non-mediated confrontation with hegemonic authority and their cultural, ideological forces. The former criticised the hegemonic structure of power and culture by theorising a form of life free from unnecessary domination in all its forms (McCarthy 1984: 7). Among others, Habermas agreed on eradicating all form of unnecessary domination and halting the colonisation of the lifeworld through a communicative rationality and discourse ethics (de Geus 2018: 7). Gramsci's model of emancipation instead depends on a paradoxical mediation between the two poles of political and cultural forces of hegemony (Laclau 2000: 48). Laclau notes how Gramsci's discrepancy with regards to Marxism touches upon the issue of emancipation of subalterns as not a result of a drastic dissolution of society in which the collapse of all particularities leaves it to be replaced by the rise of the universal achievement of general domination. On the contrary, Gramsci theorises a reconsideration about it. Hegemonic forces of both political and cultural domination happen in two spaces of confrontation: the State and the civil society (Laclau 2000: 50) through a "passive revolution", or, as Gramsci himself referred to, a "revolution-restoration".

Such "passive revolution", however, does not literally mean a state of passivity. Rather, it is a strategy of preparation for leading a certain degree of revolutionary situation(s) where in a status of pre-emerging dominancy there will be sufficient political and economic precondition(s) to replace the ruling hegemony. Unlike the majority of Marxist and de-colonial thinkers in this case, Gramsci's category of hegemony is revealed as a participative one, put at disposal of those subaltern who have to participated in, to achieve selfconsumption (Mkrtchyan 2016: 123). Thus, potential contingencies of subordination upon those who are marginalised, nameless and paperless, notfully-recognised in the wider public, have to be seen and therefore understood through a reversed angle of the socio-cultural panopticon. This unique method of coming to power puts the actors from the terrain of civil society in opposition with those of the State speaking the language of domination. This is why a perspective *from below* enables a look at the vertically imposed status of subordination, in which many cases have shown that minorities are self-aware of their own subaltern status. In this regard, any liberation struggle, or revolutionary discourse, is not denied by those who are subjected to. On the contrary, subalternity is somehow consciously performed in order to maintain a politically beneficial status quo. Aware of this, Gramsci's interpretation of hegemony cannot exclude a participation *from below* hegemony itself, and *from within* the nodes of hegemonic power apparatus. This awakening process of participation can be only understood, organised, and carried out, within the space upon which domination of hegemony is vertically imposed at first and exercised at second.

A particular example of this kind is given by Ágnes Daróczi, a Roma leader of the National Gypsy Council during the '80s in Communist Hungary, who was dismissed in August 1988 after having publicly raised a few questions to the community he belongs to in preparation for the municipal and minority elections. Questions were sent by fax with regards to practical results of establishment of minority institutions, the timetable for further coordination with the government of the majoritarian cultural system, potential regrets from within the community, achieved successes to be proud of, and the annual budget for the Roma National Government. By that time, despite cultural and political recognition of the Roma minority in Communist Hungary, Daróczi's dismissal showed nothing but that fact that the same minority group remained a flawed pariah dismissed and often forbidden in the core society due to the systematically generated relations of cultural, and not only political, relations of dominance and subordination (2018: 43). As Daróczi summed up extremely clearly, the mentality was not changed (2018: 28), and the preservation of the status quo was instrumentally maintained upon certain segments of society positioned organically on the bottom, and whose members were rendered powerless and neglected. This incapability to change mentality recalls Jacques Ricoeur's idea of historical continuity, where the idea of a consciousness perduring through history while at the same time heeding the "decentring the thinking subject" carried out by a hermeneutics of suspicion (Kearney 1999: 82).

It is here clearer why Gramsci's "Theory of Hegemony" is subtler and much more implicit than the classic understanding that Marxology and decolonial studies propel. In order to come into being (e.g., minority becoming, see Part One) a subaltern group is (un-)consciously forced to carry out a practice or behavioural pattern which becomes self-reflexive in its performativity (Olsen 2016: 122). Given this token, subordination stems thus from an implicit, external imposition, consciously carried out and brought forth by those who are affected by, whose status-formed societal identity has been imposed by an act of colonialization in time of (organic) crisis, which in turn fixates, and will maintain as such, hegemonic blocs on a cultural and political level of superiority. In this, endeavours to assert exclusive claims to a single actor's historical reliability, rather than promoting a sort of rough equality, let actors convey their claims into the wider public according to the ascribed positionality they are subjected to. After all, such positionality gives to subaltern minorities the opportunity to get benefit from it despite their silenced human condition. Because of this, minority groups cannot only be seen as social groups standing on the other side of that pre-emerging bloc which could not manage to impose itself culturally and politically while in a struggle with the one which managed to do so. It is important first and foremost to understand the subordination of minority groups in terms of cultural subordination as they are legally recognised but not accepted in the ethical field and its moral unit in society. Within this, that set of values and beliefs of the hegemonic bloc shapes collective and individual consciousness of membership and belonging to a certain force and bloc, which shapes, at the same time, political consciousness. As Gramsci had added, such political consciousness also becomes self-consciousness in which theory and practice of actions will be only one (Gramsci 1971: 133). In fact, while political hegemony is particularly close to Marxist resistance and projects of revolt/union, cultural hegemony is paramount because it overlaps not only a wealth of externally imposed concepts such as behavioural patterns, prejudices, and externally imposed discourse of stigmatization. But, such self-consciousness shaped by cultural and political hegemonic forces towards minority groups, also shapes a type of colonial understanding of the Self and of the "Other" accordingly. There are minorities that have internalised their own otherness imposed upon them; they are completely aware of it, and profit from it accordingly. Among others, a typical example could be one of Roma groups consciously involved in the so-called phenomenon of "vote selling". Interestingly enough, although they can run for democratic elections, have representative organisation on the State level (e.g., governmental platform, specific-policy plans, etc.), have freedom to express themselves, are represented on the ground (e.g., NGOs, civic movements, cross-country solidarity campaigns against their exclusion, etc.), they continue to get benefit from their subaltern and instrumental role of "vote sellers".

In this case, once again, a Gramscian perspective of hegemony in the post-Communist societies recalls a widespread notion of "post-colonial" understood in terms of human conditionality which cannot be really (arguably) undone due to related instrumental positionality. Today's struggle of newly arrived minorities (e.g., LGBTQI+, disabled, migrant communities) has beyond any doubt complicated, or perhaps rendered more confrontational the minority issues at stake. Gramsci might here warn that a wide series of polemic issues for the society and thought-provoking debates about fundamental sexual, moral, and intellectual questions challenge the political representation and functions of the parties, namely of the authorities. Yet, it is nothing but the crisis of hegemony, that is, the crisis of the State. To partially conclude, Gramsci's category of hegemony helps to not only understand the motivations behind majority mistreatments three decades onwards from the collage of the former hegemonic power, but it also demonstrates the inadequacy of "liberal" attempts of the majoritarian cultural systems at reform. In spite of well-meant ventures to present minorities favourably, majoritarian hegemony over the realm of everyday life means that the latter continues to subjugate these social groups.

CHAPTER SEVEN

Gramsci's Way Out: Subaltern Mobilisation and the Role of Intellectuals

To sum up the previous two chapters, the "organic crisis" and further domination of hegemonic leadership constitute a tandem that cannot be understood as a grave which once put in place, forever will remain. Hegemony is timeless existential, whose *a priori* logic has to be seen through the prism of a historical narrative. Hegemony itself is always led gradually indeed, shifting gears along passages that cannot be exclusively understood through an orthodox Marxist approach. On the contrary, it has to be seen through the logic of contingent struggle *for yet another* hegemonic *leadership* to come (Žižek 2017: 107). From a minority perspective, hegemony has to be participated in order to lead non-hegemonic communities to "passively revolutionise" the realm of domination they are subjected to, and replace it with another. Throughout such process of participation, which is a molecular process composed of ideological particularities to be combined into a larger formation, intellectuals are the main actors in leading what Gramsci called "war of position". The latter is not an action aimed at storming the Winter Palace and take over the power, as most of the Marxist orthodox practices could suggest. Conversely, such "war of position" reflects an everyday form of partisanism (Marchart on Gramsci 2018: 152) whose strenuous performance must unify disparate social forces and be devoted to the construction of a civil society able to lead toward a new direction in social life (e.g. common sense) and finally confront the hegemonic discourse of the State (e.g. cultural and political hegemony).

Therefore, there is here a general refusal to see minority groups as generally antagonistic due to their potential claims misleadingly understood against the structures of modern life they live in. Gramsci's structural hegemony cannot be nullified in toto indeed. It has instead to be replaced through a newly emerging political and cultural leadership coming conjecturally into dominance by letting a new terrain of confrontation emerge, where different forms of politics must be constantly formed up in order to replace the old-established hegemonic structure. This means that, according to Gramsci, one of the most relevant facets of hegemony is its reflexive mechanism of reproduction. In few words, hegemony reproduces itself by being replaced by a representative segment of society, which being previously non-hegemonic constitutes a political spin through the societal role of its élite charisma, ruling leverages, religion, and other values (e.g. historical bloc). As stated above, hegemony develops itself through its political and cultural forces only into a specific space of society, such as the Parliament or institution or neighbourhood. On the contrary, it develops itself throughout society since its intrinsically methodological mechanism constitutes a dichotomy of opposite poles: on the one hand, the leading subject towards hegemonic domination through its discourse of existence, and on the other, falling instrumentally into subordination, which has fully lacked such leadership skills. As explained above, it follows that reality becomes a matter of a discursive location, which embodies a positionality that is subjected, and melded, by the newly-arrived leadership.

To begin with, the proper question to take into account might not be the one that Spivak had raised as a *must* enquiry (1999: 270), *Can subalterns speak?* They of course can — despite the contemporary state of affairs and the deep crisis democracy is going through. It is an affirmatively unquestionable standpoint from which there is no longer a way back. On the contrary, if we would raise a philosophical enquiry over this issue, we shall raise yet other crucial questions, as follows: who speaks, and how, in the name of subaltern subjects in post-Communist Europe, in order for them to know their subaltern condition? Even more problematically, we can touch upon a paradox-within-a-paradox. Starting from Spivak's question, can we speak up on behalf of subalterns regardless of the fact that they seem reluctant to do so? Should we wait for them to speak up, in spite of the known fact that they do not own the instruments to do so?

Some postcolonial scholars have stressed the impossibility for leaders to speak on behalf of subaltern peoples as long as their intellectual status continues to tone down internal demands by keeping inferior positionality at check or to find alternative avenues to secure external resources at the expense of subalterns they want (arguably) to represent. With regard to the post-Communist region, such critique cannot dismiss the question mentioned above. On the contrary, these critiques have come out as a result of a postcolonial tendency to avoid Eurocentric ventriloquism in the protection of "subaltern rights" which end up secretly to speak on behalf of the promoters and not of the people in need. They have thus missed that, when Gramsci talks about the need for intellectuals, for example, they are instrumentally forced organically to establish a vis-à-vis relation with subalterns. It is not a matter of measuring the degree of difference or of identification between base and leadership. In the Gramscian sense, leaders need to be politically organic rather than matching "pedigree issues" from a socio-anthropological perspective. Through an empathetic "sentimental connection", intellectuals have to inscribe subaltern forms of resistance into a broader political project for emancipation and to form a new common sense in social life. The latter has thereby to find a central space to be correctly addressed and properly debated. In practice, a potential pitfall might stem from any attempt to radically awake subaltern groups against hegemonic power and authority, in which only a select group of people would have the means or inclination to participate. In the field of post-colonial studies, it is theoretically beckoned support of violently organised opposition against power and authority in forms of resistance, struggle, or reaction for anti-colonial processes of contestation against oppression of all sorts (Koskenniemri 1994: 241). Yet, similar to the act of naming and owing a definition of "cultural identity", such attempts have utterly failed due to a superficial reshuffling of both terms (Knauft 1996: 142). Gramsci instead (re-)considered resistances and subaltern cultures as politically meaningful, but only under the condition that they are integrated into a broader political project for changing the whole society. As above introduced, this counter-hegemonic participation takes the name and the form of "passive revolution", one devoted to awake consciousness of the realisation that a cleansing process and a hierarchy of values is needed to be established within the community of subalterns (Daróczi 2018: 29).

According to the subject-matter of this study, minority groups have historically faced the issue of those (self-)proclaimed spokespeople who assume their rights to speak on behalf of all members of the minority they belong to. Pretending to put their expertise at the disposal of the community, they tend instead to pursue their own personal interests, which may even consist of the perpetuation of the group in its current status of subalternity that provides them with their socially lower positionality. The formation of these potentially named "community leaders" or "community authorities", is not clear or not entirely clear with regard to how such authority comes into being (Raud 2016: 390). Once again, we have here to specify how a potential application of the category of post-coloniality does not exclusively go along with a non-mediated form of struggles for the dissolution of power structures. It rather aims to awake against subaltern conditionality externally imposed and culturally ascribed that result from a hegemonic colonisation of knowledge and imposed subordination of human condition—no matter if individual or collective. Yet, above all, the way Hall correctly underlines (1987) the necessity to shed lights once again on Gramsci's philosophy of praxis is related to the potential explanation we could get from the formation of "community leaders" and "authorities". According to Gramsci, mobilisation of intellectuals and further empowerment of subalterns have to be understood through the role of those intellectuals who are not directly connected to the existing and ruling classes throughout a given period within certain (nodal) point of space and time (Mkrtchyan 2016: 114).

Gramsci's understanding of intellectuals, which is key to better comprehend hegemony, is societally functional for the creation as well as the organisation of the consent (Gramsci 1971: 200-201). Consent is primarily necessary for embracing a new form of intellectual leadership which, in turn, challenges hegemonic conditions imposing subordination upon certain segments of society. In this regard, it shall be remarked that Gramsci's concept of hegemony is not a neutral description of what is going on in society. On the contrary, paraphrasing Laclau's pro-Gramscian contribution, it is more a descriptive analysis of the society which, if conjecturally understood, is in its turn a condition of possibility (Laclau 2000: 80). Once again, this confirms the curious character of Gramsci's Marxism along its philosophically unique contribution to the history of European Marxism. Along with the term "subaltern", Gramsci's coin of the term "intellectual" does not philosophically follow the typically old-fashioned Marxist read of concrete economic-industrial bases shaping strata between members of society. He himself divides intellectuals into two groups, "organic" and "traditional", thereby identifying different (potential of) performativity and role of leadership that may always change by coming into being (Mkrtchyan 2016: 114).

The term "intellectual" opens particularly up the philosophical debate over the definition of such term in Gramsci's vocabulary and the way Gramsci himself would have propelled it. It is firstly a complex issue which, to a certain extent, is similar to the attempt to name a taxonomy of peoplehood in relation with the notion of minorityhood. In the condensed and elliptical diction between the "organic intellectuals" and the "traditional ones", the central point does not regard only the traditionally historical category of intellectuals, but also in the proposal of Gramsci's unity of theory and practice (e.g. praxis) as a basic Marxist postulate. In this regard, both organic and traditional intellectuals do not only contribute to the terrain of the civil society, thus as economic actors through their functions. They also play a vital role in the social and political field (Gramsci 1971: 184). For example, organic intellectuals are mostly "specialised" and hold a monopoly of important, societal services: religious, educational, moral, judicial, good working ethics and so forth. However, according to Gramsci, organic intellectuals do not much refer to a particular societal group, but they are those who are traditionally considered as philosophers, writers, artists, clergy members or pedagogical figures. Nevertheless, they hold considerable economic power and socially prestigious positions in the society, they compose an élite that each social group coming into existence creates alongside itself and elaborates in case of further development. As a matter of fact, however, they remain dependent on the dominant social group in spite of their intellectual position. To a certain extent, they are those intellectuals who have preserved throughout diverse "organic crises" their symbolical and political, or even virtual, position which, in their absence, would be already directed to traditional intellectuals.

Similar to the category of hegemony, here a serious reflection of the condition of intellectuals has to be taken into account. In fact, while organic intellectuals think of themselves as "independent" and feel to be politically and culturally autonomous from hegemonic forces and endowed with a character of their own, they are nothing more than the dominant group's deputies (Gramsci 1971: 12). In other words, for Gramsci they should perform as the organisers of a collective being which is supposed to bring about a new hegemonic domination (Marchart 2018: 192), but they are the representatives of a complex organism of services which they (un)consciously reproduce since hegemonic and dominant groups need them to create conditions for the general system of relations. As Fanon noticed in post-colonial struggle in Africa in general and Algeria in particular, these organic intellectuals represent that *petite bourgeoisie* whose way of thinking has been already marked in many ways by the comparatively well-to-do-class (1967: 86). Although they seem to criticise and apparently try to awake consciousness against the upper, dominant classes, they can do so because they are the entrepreneurs (i.e. *dirigenti*) in the hands of the same dominant social groups. They only exercise societal (subaltern) positions to which they are subjugated. Their societal role can be performed if-and-only if authorised and legitimated by dominant classes. In fact, organic intellectuals generally derive from existing ruling hegemony, thanks to which their power of criticism and societal role, which they think they independently possess, has been vertically given. They are thus formed in connection with all social groups, but particularly linked more the one which has come to power, and they undergo most extensive and complex elaboration in connection with it. Although Gramsci here relegated economic determinants to the background of the "struggle stage" against existing and ruling hegemony, thereby bringing to the fore the role of intellectuals in the process of establishing consent, he himself pointed out that without economic leverage, there would be no difference between traditional and organic intellectuals. The latter cannot be recognised as such if they do not interpose themselves with the former. Paraphrasing Gramsci, organic intellectuals are members of the "party" which, as yet another literal issue in Gramsci's slippery terminology, is not used in its usual sociological sense based on the characterisation of political entities or the degree to which they confront the requirement of their political typologies. In contrast, party (i.e. *partito*) signifies the primacy of the superstructure over the structure. Hence, it follows that organic intellectuals are authorised and legitimised by traditional intellectuals in their actions within the societal structure, representing social groups they super-structurally belong to, or have been ascribed, and from which they organically derive. Hence, traditional intellectuals are those linked to the social masses, those not belonging eventually to the petite bourgeoisie, not yet elaborated and set in motion by capitalist system. In fact, peasantry was for Gramsci the main group of traditional intellectuals to refer to. They respect the socio-cultural role of organic intellectuals, but sometimes they show contempt for them, which means that this admiration is oftentimes mingled with instinctive elements of envy and impassioned anger.

We might hence consider extremely valid the critique of the error to distinguish intellectuals in accordance with the intrinsic nature of their intellectual activities (Kearney and Rainwater 1996: 186). What appears a traditional and vulgarised type of distinction cannot be considered as a line by which intellectuals and non-intellectual actions can be differentiated one from another, and whether or not actions of intellectual elaborations regard to muscular-nervous or culture-oriented effort. Indeed, the distinction between organic and traditional intellectuals in the ensemble of the system of relation and group-dynamics has to point out how they contribute to maintain subaltern positions through their activities. The latter stems from the externally ascribed positionality they (un)consciously hold within the same social groups they have been created by, ascribed to, and often neglected from. In fact, as Gramsci pointed clearly out, all men are intellectuals since the *homo faber* – namely, a person able to create – cannot be detached from the *homo sapiens* (Kearney and Rainwater 1996: 187).

Given this token, a look beneath at what Gramsci sociologically analysed, the issue regarding subalterns' "enjoyment" of hegemonic elements becomes self-explanatory. In sum, Gramsci pointed out how hegemonic leadership must throw subalterns out of joint moment in order to secure its position of domination. In relation with the dichotomy of organic and traditional intellectuals among subaltern groups, the subject matter of this study gives credit to the socio-cultural analysis of the Italian thinker. Attempts to confront Gramsci's role of intellectual across contemporary CEE immediately brings up a deeper, perhaps socially clearer, perspective of the main reasons why minority groups have utterly failed to mobilise themselves positively instead of remaining a major concern. In the last few years, for instance, minority groups have had opportunities to improve their status[1] and everyday condition. While many argue that they have managed to adapt to new circumstances, others point out how lack of both capacity and advocacy skills has limited their influence on policy-making processes. This double-edged context of professionalisation of politics (Wunsch 2018: 47) is nothing but the reluctance of representatives of minority groups — traditional intellectuals in Gramsci's language — to trigger, or at least partially agree on, substantive actions of change on the ground. Especially those recognised by self-embodiment and gatherings of societal groups along ethnic or religious features, have never managed to represent themselves, either politically or even culturally, through intellectual figures of change. They have more likely played a "logic of consequences" (March and Olsen 1998) whereby their socio-political actions have been oriented to behave only strategically in ways aimed at maximising their power and benefits. By speculation, an opposite scenario would further mean a risk for their own privileges (Wunsch 2018: 2). In Bulgaria, for example, the abovementioned Movement for Rights and Freedoms (MRF) has been depicted as an "enigma-within-an-enigma" (Leviev-Sawyer 2015) because of its position within the political spectrum and socio-cultural positionality of representation on the ground among ethno-religious minority members. Similarly, the main Serb minority political party in Kosovo, Srpska Lista (Serbian List), has always played the role of representative entity of Serbia-promoted interference in the country. Permanent in the northern areas and also overwhelming in the central, southern and eastern regions of Kosovo, Serbian List remains the only organisation which is allowed to keep a certain political performativity thanks to the Albanian hegemonic power structures in Kosovo, without which the role of the Serbian minority could not be the way it currently is. In South Caucasus, the Karabakhi-Armenian leadership that resulted from the First War (1992–1994) is nothing but the result of the postwar scenario where post-Soviet

---

[1] For instance, the Stabilisation and Association Agreement (SAAs), which regulates access of candidate countries to access the European Union, means a lot for Western Balkan minority groups since the regulation contains straight mechanism of obligations and conditionality to Candidate State regarding full recognition and protection of minority rights, of refugees and returnees, and kin-state relations.

Armenian hegemonic structures of politics and culture came into existence within a region which continues to be considered a de facto State. In parallel, the role of organic intellectuals confirms what Gramsci had pointed out. By being recognised as minority groups' members, and by being engaged in the sphere of education and culture (e.g. recognition of cultural claims, bilingual schooling system, territorial autonomy), organic intellectuals are the ones reproducing hegemonic ideologies (Mkrtchyan 2016: 115) and stiffening their hidden power structures, without which their subaltern status cannot exist and be recognised. The organisation they say to speak in praise of, for those people they say to speak on behalf of, are a trade union of individual interests rather than a type of organisation which, in Gramsci's sense, ought to make possible a free exchange of ideas and actions reflecting the needs of subalterns (Fanon 2011: 89). According to the three case studies, in Bulgaria the so-called "Turkish electoral tourism" across Bulgaria and Turkey, or the "Roma vote sellers" phenomenon within the country, are two sides of the enigmatic status of MRF's representatives (traditional intellectuals) over those people they aim to represent, within the Bulgarian arena polluted by political corruption on the political and cultural ground. Among Kosovo Serbs, those who subtly reinforce ethnic identity-based cultural claims while engaging in political actions are evidently those who benefit from the Serbia-promoted parallel system within Kosovo, out of which they are able to make their living (Trupia and Schwandner-Sievers 2019). According to the third example, KarabakhiArmenians are those who continue to pay the highest price of today's ruling élites and their purposeful lack of political motivations and wills to definitely compromise (Ayunts, Zolyan, and Zakaryan 2016). In this regard, the realm of everyday life sheds more light on the subtle function of hegemonic structures. While a post-Communist organic crisis lasts, emergence of political and cultural hegemonic blocs continues to give opportunity to traditional intellectuals to struggle, apparently. Under the parapet of such hegemonic power relations, subaltern groups are allowed to exist, be recognised, and performed, because they have been conquered ideologically. In this regard, while traditional intellectuals are fully assimilated, simultaneously elaborated, and culturally digested by yet another subaltern group composed of organic intellectuals (Gramsci 1971: 10), postCommunist management of resources of power has so far provided and created models and methods of cultural autonomy and political representation without ceasing subordination.

In order to interrupt this (behaviour) pattern, which results from subtle and implicit forms of hegemonic mechanisms of exclusion, Gramsci's philosophy of praxis highlights how not all intellectuals are directly connected to the existing and ruling political and cultural hegemonic structures. Their real task and societal role to perform does not diverge much from that of criticising, whining, and replacing the hegemonic blocs through a cultural awakening process. This is without any doubt centrally paramount for leading the way toward a path of dominance whose further, final stage would reach the replacement of hegemony. Gramsci's analysis is here twofold. On the one hand, the role of intellectuals cannot be understood in the commonly considered idea of "intellectualism". On the other hand, rather than traditional intellectuals, organic intellectuals are Gramsci's quicker and more efficacious group in question for succeeding to elaborate its own historical bloc at first, in order to assimilate and conquer "ideologically" the traditional intellectuals afterwards (Gramsci 1971: 10). Through such perspective, Gramsci's Marxism, which remains such in theory as well as in praxis—is definitely at the disposal of subalterns. It may thereby follow that any social replacement of hegemony integrates the most marginal communities and further begins with their spontaneous forms of politics, shaping a historical bloc (e.g., leading process) into a political initiative (e.g., consent) where certain elements of hegemony undergo hegemony itself. In other words, Gramsci called for a philosophy of praxis in order to elevate popular resistances to a higher degree of politicisation. The latter begins not with the involvement of traditional intellectuals, who are members of phenomena that ensure social-political equilibrium or, in case of their absence, consolidate various realities (Mkrtchyan 2016: 114). They brought organic intellectual into prominence for the instrumental purpose of hegemony structures. In fact, traditional intellectuals are as such because they act according to a general conception of life they have received (e.g. common sense), one of philosophical meanings and explanations whose dignity provides principles of differentiation from older, ruling ideologies. It gives a (hegemonic) recognition through a pedagogical imprinting based on a scholastic, along with a pedagogical programme of education, of which traditional intellectuals are oftentimes part. Therefore, if and only if there is an objective to form a new hegemony, organic intellectuals have to take responsibility and provide a newly appropriate value system by using their creativity.

In general, this explains why the latest projects of liberation struggles, feminist revolt, poststructuralist destabilisation, remain exclusively an option (e.g., de-colonial alternative), which is far from Gramsci's practical roadmap. Their non-mediated frontal interpretation of liberation actions against hegemonic power structures, which are paradoxically theorised more by traditional intellectuals rather than organic ones, tend to present subalterns as social entities to empower in order to let them fulfil the task of presenting logical contradictions of their realm of subordination. Such "nonmediated reconciliation" with hegemony, like Marx's philosophy of praxis, has historically stressed a constitution of true emancipation (Laclau 2000: 47) among the orthodox tradition of Marxology. Unlike Gramsci's philosophy of praxis, this remains an illusive task that cannot overtake the real Gramsci's proposal: a construction of a new ideology whose articulation has to configure different subjects, different identities, different projects, and different aspirations in order to construct a "unity" out of difference. In other words, Gramsci's call for the construction of a counter-hegemonic discourse and action brings both organic as well as traditional intellectuals to become not members of imagined communities of resisters; neither, as Hall provocatively argued, to write books (1987) nor present themselves as men of letters, philosophers or artists (Kearney and Rainwater 1996: 187). Rather, they have to be considered as a community of "awakeners" devoted to promote their ideas (Hobsbawm 1983, quoted by Dawson 2016: 11) through a dissemination of their narratives in ever-widening discursive arenas. If in the eyes of Gramsci everyone is an intellectual (1971) because equipped with intellectual capacities, intellectuals are therefore those who simply have to calculate their ideas in order to be aware of how to survive, how to look after those other people they are close to, with whom they have interests to pursue and keep connections with in their everyday life, and so on. Each man and each woman can represent and ensure the triumph of the action carried out in his or her locality. In other words, as Fanon pointed out, they represent subaltern knowledge composed of all voices, interests, values and perspectives, which are rendered subaltern and dismissed from the public sphere. Although ascribed as inferior and/or secondary by the asymmetric mechanism that hegemony shapes within the realm of existence, they can always constitute a discourse of liberation (2011: 105).

However, remaining stably in the field of revolutionary actorness, Gramsci does not reject in toto the potential of traditional intellectuals. On the contrary, despite the fact that they tend to cultivate their self-image of isolated minds, they can organise together with organic intellectuals a collective being by implicating themselves into their being-in-the-world in terms of their being-in-the-political (Marchart 2018: 192). Although their traditional organisations of all kind intensify warning against organic intellectuals and organisation, they are pivotal for contesting, winning, and further replacing the hegemony they are subjected to. Traditional intellectuals know very well that ideas and projects presented to them are more likely introduced to keep control over their agency since they do not question the real nature of unchanging, everlasting subordination and knowledge exploitation. Especially in CEE, this happens when subaltern traditional members – namely ordinary people – are taken only in consideration by a system of empowerment and services of knowledge functioning only into an a priori schedule (Fanon 2011: 89). Nevertheless, their traditonal forms of participation within hegemony constitutes a historical bloc which speaks out their own culture and reorganisation of power structure. To a certain extent, it seems that Gramsci's presentation of intellectual vanguard has to sneak in the political and cultural hegemonic structures as Trojan Horse-like leadership; once inside, they would easily disentangle and defeat nodal points of hegemony by replacing them on a political and cultural ground, and finally winning them.

Among others, one of the examples to take here into account is the long trajectory of Kosovo Albanians in Yugoslavia. In a Gramscian sense, the 1999 Kosovo War was historically anticipated by a nonviolent mobilisation of intellectual figures. Ibrahim Rojana, for instance, eschewed the national liberation struggle to create a parallel civil society where a large part of the population actively participated with peaceful campaigns, such as in 1989 for the Trepça miners' strike. Despite the cruelty of ethnic cleanings, the Kosovo Albanian "counter-revolution" occurred peacefully. The rejection of Kosovo's status of autonomy in support of a sovereign Republic of Kosovo was the first contestation against Belgrade, which attempted to impose a new status of autonomy or highly territorial partition and ethnic segregation on Kosovo.

According to the subject-matter of this study, a real dissolution of subaltern positionality so far explained passes not by a revolutionary momentum, nor by an implementation of new top-down approaches (e.g., normative) aiming at destroying *tout court* the minority status, thereby empowering certain segments of a minority rather than another. In Gramsci's prospective realm, intellectuals of minority groups are more likely owners of "subjected knowledge", previously rendered culturally inferior and politically secondary. The real task remains here to achieve a socio-cultural emancipation and intellectual recognition within their own socially marginalised community first, and making their group of discourse and existence become hegemonic, second. In order to do so, the Italian thinker pointed out a philosophical roadmap through which intellectuals have to lead the way for a new space of discourse and existence, in which, between the asymmetric structure that hegemony shapes by dividing society and ruling over, intellectuals navigate *coercion* and *consent* for providing a newly appropriate values system. In other words, the societal role of intellectuals is to create and drive themselves a force towards a new knowledge to come into domination; a way for disentangling stagnation of hegemonic status quo and ceasing with a negative awareness of subordination subaltern groups are consciously part of. Thus, intellectuals have to fulfil the crucial task of creating new ideological terrain in order to determine a reform of consciousness and methods of new knowledge (Gramsci 1971:365–366); namely, a new consciousness released from the nodal points of the hegemonic state of affairs, a new method to see and represent collective identities and awake them.

Following Gramsci's relevance given to intellectual leadership, in CEE weak political mobilisation among minority groups seems analogous to the "heaven to hell" situation in the public sphere (Wunsch 2018:33). Gramsci's perspective is helpful to investigate the relationship between marginal communities and intellectuals, political leaders or social movements and organisations, from within. On a cultural level, traditional (minority) intellectuals face the dilemma of an asymmetry of interests to pursue with organic (minority) intellectuals. What seems to be one of the consequences and phenomena of hegemony, is practically manifested in the distrust of any form of political leadership, which is perceived as paradoxically "different" from people's needs and interests to be represented. Among minority groups, studies show that minority élites in Southeast Europe either tone down internal demands or find different avenues to secure resources (2018:163). During political campaings, many exceed in promising something they know they cannot guarantee. This, which the essence of the promise in-itself (Rancière 1994), remains at the same time the *telos* of the community they speak in praise of. In this regard, networks, interests, socio-economic conditions, and cultural capital diverge from those traditional (minority) intellectuals that organic (minority) intellectuals intend (or oftentimes pretend) to represent. This is why, as Rancière pointed out, those splintered parts of the same community rain back down like murderous stones (1994:5). On a political level, for example, some organic intellectuals have emerged as leaders of social (subaltern) organisations with the intention of representing groups with lower opportunities. Yet, processes of professionalisation have followed, institutionalising intra-society relations (Wunsch 2018:33) in which there is no longer an exchange of ideas elaborated according to the real needs of the peoples, but transformed into a trade union of individual interests (Fanon 2011). Thereby, antagonistic mediation against hegemons are basically nullified and paradoxically oriented within the relations of organic and traditional intellectuals. As a matter of fact, both result from a directly manifested phenomenon of hegemony, which vertically imposes an ethical and moral asymmetry by vacuuming a spatial limbo in between a certain allowed performativity of subalternity, regulated by law and discursively justified, and restrictions of other forms of performativity, which are forbidden to avoid any mobilisation of groups and further creation of dominance capable of replacing hegemony itself by leading a yet new one. This imposed asymmetry, in which Wunsch noticed through the prism of professionalisation of politicians and institutionalisation within State relations, is nothing but the condition that, according to Gramsci, subalterns tend to enjoy by being part of the hegemony structures they are subjected to. It is, in the very end, the salient representation of the two poles of society, namely State and civil society, which Gramsci saw in opposition and confrontation between each other because leading-entities of that *conditio sine qua non* hegemony can arise from or be contested, won and replaced.

So far, inclusion and empowerment of minority groups into the "core society" have been presented through strategies at work in the middle of the public sphere, a space in between political institutions and the broader population. In Gramsci's language, the State speaks by the language of its specific epoch, while the civil society constitutes itself as a political space (Laclau 2000: 48). Without any doubt, Gramsci's civil society is the space for intellectuals leading into dominance. It is not only a space from where opportunities for mobilisation might emerge, but it is also a space on which vis-à-vis confrontation between the State (hegemony)/civil society (subaltern positionality) occurs, leaving room to critical voices to be organised into a political dimension through which group's dominance might come into being and replace ruling and existing hegemony with its own hegemony of discourse and existence.

CHAPTER EIGHT
The Paradox of Hegemonic (In-)Tolerance

In the attempt to further (re-)examine the three aspects of Gramscian philosophy above introduced, the principle of tolerance is one of the much debated issues we can take into account. In fact, the latter is centrally paramount in contemporary democracies, particularly those where minority groups play a central role from within. In order to follow up the proposed Didi-Huberman's vision of coexistent people and its implicit category of coexistence, along with Gramsci's category of hegemony understood as leadership, limits and paradoxes of tolerance have recently begun to question the model of liberal multicultural. Among others, Will Kymlicka, one of the most influential political philosopher of our times (König 2001: 48), who has extensively written and philosophically contributed to the subject-matter, is useful as a point of reference and for critical comparison at the same time.

From this point of view, Will Kymlicka's Theory of Minority Rights and Liberal Multiculturalism represents a milestone in academia despite widespread critiques towards the approach that the Canadian philosopher has theorised, developed and applied over different contexts. Across multiple influential publications, Kymlicka asserts that the demand for group rights is often phrased in terms of tolerance (1992: 39) pointing also to the need for diverse forms of tolerance. In this regard, he pays particular attention to two specific models of toleration in connection with religion and religious communities. In general, Kymlicka's political philosophy seeks to guarantee integration and inclusion to all sub-groups regardless of their ethnocultural features and territories they live in. In other words, his attempts to channel marginalised and unrecognised groups into a roadmap aimed at softening clashes and guaranteeing rights in the larger society follow up Charles Taylor's Politics of Recognition and Michael Sandel's communitarianism.

By doing so, Kymlicka differentiates national minorities from immigrant communities along ethno-cultural lines in the attempt to facilitate policy making to allocate minority rights and increase cultural understanding among and within diverse populations, avoiding negative impact on the longterm Western tradition of political liberalism (Rawls, 1993). In particular, allocation of specific-group rights cannot contrast the individual freedom of conscience and autonomy of individuals since they are foundational. Regardless of national minorities or immigrant communities, tolerance toward minority groups can only be endorsed as long as minority groups desire to survive in a culturally distinct society. Within this, the right to maintain a minority membership and protect that culture from the majoritarian cultural system is guaranteed in the same way, and as long as, members of majority culture are able to maintain and develop theirs. This "as long as" is clearly the degree of tolerance within which minority desires to live culturally distinct lives within the larger society cannot inherently connect the desire to maintain a distinct societal culture with a self-organised form of isolation (Kymlicka and Opalski, 2000: 75). Nonetheless, the numerous challenges of the so-called "century of migrants" (Nail 2015) brought Kymlicka to distinguish national minorities from communities of newcomers by drawing a line along ethno-cultural features of both minority groups. While members of national minorities belong to distinct cultural groups from the larger society of the State in which they live—territorially concentrated, usually homogenous, formerly selfgoverning, institutionally complete, and entitled to those rights of selfgovernance which are seen as inherent rights—immigrants compose more heterogeneous communities within the host-State where they seek refuge and humanitarian protection. On the one hand, presence at the time of a State's foundation and prior to the historical experience of self-government, along with common culture, common language, and self-governance through their institutions—all should guarantee rights to self-determination for national minorities. On the other hand, immigrant communities are composed of heterogeneous groups of people who have decided to "voluntarily" move from their country of origin; therefore they cannot campaign for and seek the same cultural and political prospects to which national minorities are entitled. Unlike national minorities, immigrant communities do not possess "societal culture" in the host-State—namely, a set of pre-conditional measures and unique situations. While national minorities can endorse governments and influence the political agenda since they have been (forcedly) incorporated, either by historical conquests or hierarchical power changes, immigrant communities can neither recreate nor claim a set of institutions along with cultural practices and heritage they once had and performed in their countries of origin. After all, even with generosity and toleration (as Kymlicka openly states), immigrant communities represent a small and dispersed minority group across different host-States. Such a distinction has to be clear among lawmakers and international organisations whose work aims at avoiding cultural misunderstandings among and within immigrant communities. In fact, Kymlicka does not distinguish national minorities from immigrant groups to allocate group rights to the firsts and deny them to the seconds. Kymlicka here wishes to go deeper in identifying ethno-cultural features of immigrant communities in order to not to leave room for banal forms of nationalism and its vernacular politics[1].

Nonetheless, the whole classification is beyond doubt problematic because, putting aside the theoretical context, it overlooks the real-life ground in which a large number of members belonging to immigrant communities might not have the right to hold citizenship and consider their life completely different from that of the host-State. Perhaps highly conditioned by a Canadian background, Kymlicka considers immigrant communities to be "loose associations" that do not occupy their historical land of origin on the one hand; but, he does not pay much attention to the societal ties such communities are capable to shape once having arrived in the host-State. In so doing, Kymlicka not only tends to simplify the realm of everydayness related particularly to further societal paradigms of coexistence, therefore of tolerance between immigrant community and majority members in the "West"—he simplifies the real cultural traumas that (may) affect personal or collective identity of a societal group: dislocations from country of origin to the host-State, which go even beyond all potential inclusion policies, and (may) cause fragmentation of the Self and of the Othering. At first glance, Kymlicka takes for granted the attitude of the majority toward resilience and tolerance for both new-coming and pre-existing Otherness from within its cultural context. When Kymlicka suggests the inclusion of immigrant communities through the acquisition of the host-State language, he surprisingly ignores how language per se is a vague criterion for being considered a "cultural maker" for an acquaintance of a set of cultural signifiers and signified that (most probably) immigrants would neither wholly accept nor unreservedly uphold (Glavanakova 2016: 111-114).

More than language, the above-mentioned distinction should shed light on how tolerance plays a role in the everyday relations of majority and minority communities. Hence, legal restriction upon immigrant groups to claim cultural rights would paradoxically take the risk to trigger marginalisation and exclusion for those who do not succeed in integrating themselves into the larger society. In turn, as Kymlicka points

---

[1] Kymlicka identifies immigrant communities whose members may have (i) the right to become citizen, (ii) those who do not have such right, and (iii) refugees. See also Dmytro Hys (2004): 35.

out, the majoritarian cultural system will not reduce its (unconscious) desire to present itself as natural, completed, monolithic and standardised Nation-State. Also, for national minorities—for whom a proposal for self-governing rights aims at ensuring that they will not become outbids for the greater wealth of outsiders (Kymlicka and Marìn, op. cit., p. 137) from neighbouring kinStates—Kymlicka focuses only on federal power distribution. Hence, Kymlicka suggests an asymmetrical representation, namely an asymmetrical power distribution in the attempt to strengthen the multicultural character of a State. Among others, language policy and rights of self-governance are best allocated and protected through a form of multinational federalism, thereby allowing the creation of regional politics in the hands of national minority political organisations along with their substantial (and constitutionally protected) power of self-government. In other words, in Kymlicka's sense, tolerance should be guaranteed within a federation of generally concentrated peoples or nations whose boundaries have been drawn and their power distributed in such a way that each national group will maintain itself as a distinct and self-government societal culture (Kymlicka and Opalski, 2000: 269). Although Kymlicka seems here to suggest a model of toleration by trying to shape social unity and (in the end) a desire to live together, he overlooks the everyday conditions under which sub-national and immigrant communities will be capable of seeking recognition and further coexistence with the majoritarian cultural system. For example, the majority-minority state of affairs in many Eastern European countries is the result of a sediment repository of historical struggles for power and existence, which has come to symbolise and signify cultural and political hegemonic hierarchies among societal groups.

Here one may be in agreement with Seyla Benhabib and her criticism that remarks how such distinction between national and immigrant minority groups is possible to draw along ethno-cultural features on the one hand, but it overlooks everyday attitude of people toward Otherness on the other hand. Within the vacuum which makes Kymlicka's theory highly descriptive but not normative, the Canadian philosopher came to affirm that the Ottoman Millet system was the most developed form of the group rights model in terms of religious tolerance (Kymlicka, op. cit., p.38). Similarly, Terian seems to follow up. She noticed how national movements that resulted from the Ottoman Empire, as well as Austro-Hungarian domination, managed to develop themselves from a high degree of cultural independence they possessed. Terian hence affirmed how such independence is comparable with the self-determination of ethnic groups, present in different nations within a State, despite the fact they did not have any administration autonomy.

Although Kymlicka does not stand for it, as a Rawlsian and supporter of the neutrality of the liberal State in defence of individual liberty within plural societies, Kymlicka highlights the many regimes, including contemporary democracies such as Canada, the United States, and Great Britain, have asked for and reproduced implementation of Millet-style model. In fact, it is not surprising that some Muslim leaders have called for a Millet-style system in Britain, one which would allow Muslims to govern themselves according to their own laws regarding education and family status. Kymlicka is here aware of the cultural paradox and political challenge the State faces by trying to balance itself in defence of liberal values and allocation of group rights that often deny the liberal principle of individual freedom of conscience the same liberal State stands for.

The paradox here is twofold. First, any kind of denials or restrictions of group rights against national minorities and immigrant communities cannot be justified by the State through the prism of its liberal values, what John Rawls legitimates as benign neglect. Paradoxically, Rawls's and Kymlicka's idea of political liberalism (which stands for the recognition of specific marginalised groups) cannot be justified while the State denies or restricts opportunities it stands for. Hence, justifications and consequences of a potentially imposed benign neglect over a minority practice cannot be entirely neutral in the sense of equally denying claims and restricting performativity of some cultural rights. In practice, it would not be possible for the State to handle disloyal behaviour of a specific minority group in identifying dissident voices that from within succeed in remaining free to question, revise or reject communitarian practices and values.

In particular, if we affirm that each individual differs in which cultural elements she decides to choose, adopt, or internalise (Glavanakova 2016: 47), differentiations in personal experiences of cultural exchange and interaction inside and outside the community she belongs to, we should agree that each human subject can lead herself to multiple interpretations of values and practices. In turn, it would be hard for the State to act properly with the purpose to recognise and allocate group rights only according to internal dissidents who reject disloyalty while trying to protect isolationist and illiberal communities they belong to. This would lead the State to cease its liberal principle of non-interference since the benign neglect would come to force by valuing cases differently and only then acting accordingly.

Second, recognition of diverse forms of religious toleration—which

Kymlicka supports as long as they are plausible—would be difficult to achieve in practice. For example, it would be almost impossible for the State to restrict specific-group rights to those Muslims asking for self-governance regarding family law and schooling system while identifying liberal Muslims who have signed a *fatwa*[2] issued against the Islamic State in order to guarantee protection of their cultural rights in support of liberal values. In fact, minority groups cannot be understood as monolithic from within, but as minorities within which sub-groups intersect. What are the possibilities for recognising and protecting the rights of LBGTQI+ Muslims who desire to continue their worship in spite of facing threats for having questioned orthodox interpretations of Islamic doctrine, such as heresy or apostasy? More than ever, minority groups are "under fire" due to intersectional aspects that are turning rigidly old-fashioned parameters of labelling such social groups into more dynamic segment of the population.

Kymlicka's approach towards minority groups seems generally plausible as it strengthens his philosophical argumentation in Multicultural Citizenship (1995) without raising, at least in theory, major concerns. While Kymlicka's theory is beyond doubt a serious attempt to soften cultural misunderstanding in societies that are on the verge of radically changing, his taking-for-grantedness over cultural issues of minority groups impinges on the potential implementation of his theoretical framework on the ground. According to the post-Communist Europe, one should agree on the fact that post-1989 deterioration of highly ideological messages for subalterns across Western Europe in parallel with the three-decade-long demise of the Eastern Bloc has paradoxically left room for the rise of illiberal forms of democracy along the majoritarian cultural lines rather than minority claims. For example, Kymlicka and others have begun to sustain approaches that have never won ground but instead gripped, and perhaps purposefully developed, over politics in vernacular. Return to modern forms of nationalism bolstered negative attitudes toward Otherness, feeding upon each other in what experts name in terms of population. To this end, there is thus an extreme need to (re-)examine and (re-)consider how forms of tolerance and models of toleration would pursue realisation. In general, one should restart reconsidering the everyday practices of tolerance, rather than, as Kymlicka has done so far, trying to modulate or set up models of toleration which remain paradoxically too far from the real-life situations in which people face each other by living, coexisting, or

---

[2] Within the tradition of the Islamic law (sharia), a fatwa is a nonbinding legal opinion regarding a specific issue raised by a qualified jurist in order to address a private manner or also a specific aspect of governance.

arguing together.

Here, not only liberals have failed in their attempts to readjust societies by imposing values of tolerance and mutual respect, but it is also the leftist approach from the radical to the liberal spectrum that has utterly failed in defending what they proclaim to defend and stand for. For example, Jean-Luc Melanchon's recent proposal to defend French minorities within a people considered "one and indivisible" in France turns out to be a different form of assimilation within the institutional framework constituting the French State, its dominant culture, its "national" history, and its norms (Khiari 2016: 96). What Khiari notices through the prism of a culturally unbiased assumption of the Left Front had been, as above introduced, noticed by Antonio Gramsci, who had highlighted how the State presents itself in the language and culture of its specific epoch through imposing its cultural hegemony over civil society in tandem with its hierarchically political hegemony. In addition, Kymlicka also anticipated how such assumptions came to be misleading for Marxists as much as liberals. To put it into philosophical speculation, Kymlicka notes that just as how Mill said that the Quebecois should accept assimilation into the majority English-speaking culture of Canada, so Marx said the Czech should integrate into German culture (Kymlicka and Rubio 1999: 136). Thus, not only liberal models of toleration but also leftist consideration, which should be ideologically alternative to liberal suggestion, process along assimilation policies that signify in concrete terms the exclusion of the excluded. While liberals maintain their perverse incentive to destroy national minority cultures (Kymlicka and Marín 1999: 140), leftists have so far contributed to preserving the status of noncitizens from subaltern groups due to their ambition to "integrate" them into the "one people" (Khiari 2016:96). For the purpose of this study, an analysis of what Kymlicka refers to as "societal culture" has to be compared through the prism of Gramsci's theory of hegemony, where a visible contrast of philosophical approaches with Kymlicka arises. By trying to (re)define tolerance and how its limits constantly unfold in contemporary liberal democracies, tolerance can be (re)considered through Gramsci's philosophy of praxis whose application over a potential model of-and-for toleration would focus on the performativity of tolerance rather than a top-down approach over majority-minority relations, as that of Kymlicka seems to be. The above-mentioned philosophical contribution of Gramsci to culture and subalternity suggests how to address "tolerance" from within the broadly differentiated forms of political as well as cultural hegemony. While the first relates to the material power of dominant ruling elites, the second is much subtler form of control over society which can be formed within what Gramsci identifies in the realm of ideology. Within this, hegemonic asymmetries made instrumentally up throughout society and manifest by imposition of certain moral values and practices of tolerance, are known because reflective production of the cultural hegemony. The latter, indeed, allows specific forms of toleration instead of others in order to recognise societal groups and maintain other into subaltern positions. In this, as Žižek has extensively written about, we deal within the field of ideology – namely, a terrain on which implicit unspoken regulations have as a rule a non-reflected relationship: something that is spontaneously tolerated in discredit of something else, that is at the same time driven by ideological imposition, put at work at its purest. Following Žižek's quote of Louis Althusser, this domain of tolerance is the domain of ideology and its functional apparatus along with its imposed practices; a domain which, now according to a less slippery Kantian terminology, allows individuals to "schematise" moral and legal norms, to make them part of their living experiences (Žižek 2017: 230).

Under these circumstances, the supremacy of hierarchically hegemonic groups performs itself through "domination," an intellectual and moral form of leadership, thereby maintaining specific aspects of everyday life in which they are trapped. Hence, it should be questioned to what extent, and most importantly how, our full-fledged democratic States (our majoritarian cultural system of which they are composed) are supposed to fully grant access to minority groups to the public realm. So far, liberal democracies have justified restriction to minority groups and forced them to relinquish their claims to guarantee sufficient levels of security in our time of terrorism and suspicion over Islam, or also tackling in advance potential turmoil that might impinge on and erupt from within the society.

It might be worth expressing how liberal values and principles continue to animate an old-fashioned struggle for liberalism and democracy against disloyal and undemocratic behaviour. However, liberal democracies—whose de jure model of tolerance vanishes on a passive acceptation and ratification of international conventions and legal documents within national legal frameworks—have ceased to even do so. The Bulgarian case related to the Istanbul Convention is self-explanatory. As a result, tolerance-related issues, such as levels of marginalisation and exclusion that minorities have never stopped to face, have become more visible. In fact, among other facets of our society, tolerance is today performed according to a set of moral values and practices whose political and intellectual manifestations take roots within nodal points that hegemonic power structure continue to regulate, and around which political correctness and masked defence of liberal values have anchored political discourses and cultural practices.

Whether or not for Kymlicka cultural interchange does not undermine the claim that there are distinct societal cultures (Kymlicka 1995:105), as Benhabib criticized Gramsci's approach over hegemonic power structures throws better light on the imposed cultural and political (pre-)disposition toward a specific phenomenon, such as tolerance. With regard to it, the notion of hegemony is thus more than a useful category to look at contemporary models of toleration, or lack of it. In times of uncertainty in which majoritarian cultural systems show illiberal attitudes through people's lost capacity to live together with Others, such an absence of willingness mirrors both intellectual and societal set of values and norms whose political articulation, historical consolidation and cultural imposition have taken roots around hegemonic nodal points. The latter is (clearly) recognisable with regard to much-discussed scenario of immigrant communities in Western Europe (e.g., Spain, France, Italy, Germany, and the US) as much as across the CEE (e.g., Poland, Hungary, Serbia, Bulgaria, and recently Ukraine) over national minorities' states of affairs.

Under these circumstances, it could be easy to justify the whole state of affairs through "members vs. rights" dilemma. In retrospect, it could be even easier to affirm that liberal States and West-style democracies could welcome a higher number of immigrants if the latter would be less committed to seeking multicultural rights, such as access to citizenship. It could also be legitimate to state that Southeast European national minorities could best achieve recognition insofar as they show readiness to relinquish self governing rights in contested territories in respect of those repositories of historical struggles that have culturally influenced majority cultural systems. However, here, I think that rather than trying to passively analyse the status quo or questioning the long-term effect on the acceptance of a model of toleration of illiberal norms and practices, it is first worth retrieving what type of tolerance liberal democracies want to respond to. More likely, within which boundaries everyday practices of tolerance will be allowed to be performed, and how (il)liberal democracies will defend them to be applied over real-life situations.

In order to understand so, it should be investigated how hegemonic nodal points are culturally imposing themselves over society shape a set of both values and norms to maintain a division between subaltern and ruling groups. Because of this, understanding how hegemony dominates and denies transformation of society means to be capable to disentangle those moral and intellectual values (e.g., nodal points) around-and-within which contemporary models of toleration are allowed to be performed while others are not. In other words, unravelling hegemonic blocs means to understand the logic of hegemony—namely, how hegemony imposes itself over society. To give an example, Kymlicka's positive consideration of the Millet-style system. By doing so, he lacks understanding of conjunctional points of the Millet system around which everyday capability among diverse communities to tolerate Others did not refer to the real state of affairs on the ground. This would therefore explain how the long-term legacy of the Millet-style system has historically left room for other cultural and political hegemonic power structures to arise which, from literature to history, continue to have negative references toward national minority and immigrant communities in the Ottoman successor States. In fact, without this deep understanding, identification of what Kymlicka labels as the best model of religious tolerance could also overlook how the Ottoman principle of tolerance was allowed to be performed only on the surface of interethnic and interfaith relations among the Ottoman population. In Gramsci's sense, we should look deeply at the Ottoman hegemonic blocs to understand the Turkic Ottoman-run system. Toleration did not fully grant recognition and coexistence indeed. On the contrary, tolerance was superficially based on an intellectual willingness of the dominant religious group to coexist with others Braude and Lewis, 1982a: 3). This is why Kymlicka overlooks how Ottoman domination really functioned, which can be similarly combined with the way the Church ruled in the Middle Age (Gramsci, op. cit.).

With regard to the Ottoman model of toleration, tolerance could not trigger—if really legitimised within the diverse population—those historically proven high levels of conversions to Islam occurring among nonMuslim communities that wanted to avoid discrimination in terms of taxation policy or pursuing interests that Turkish Ottomans secured for equal groups to balance their domestic affairs. If the Ottoman model of tolerance were studied by looking through the hegemonic power structure, as Gramsci would suggest, it would be easier to understand how everyday performativity of interfaith tolerance was lacking because neither able to penetrate people's consciousness nor able to shape real practices of tolerance. In fact, the contrary would not make historical sense in front of the mass-killings and planned ethnic cleansings that Ottoman Turks committed against Christian populations (e.g., Armenians, Greeks, Bulgarians, Serbs, Assyrians, etc.) that began even before the collapse of their Empire. From this historical perspective, the Millet-style administration model would be better described through the neologism "sultanism" that Max Weber coined—namely, a curious mixture of modern and patrimonial elements that decayed when they entrenched themselves at the expense of the modern ones. The model of toleration Kymlicka confuses in terms of religious diversity was thereby a clearly hegemonic power instrument of control at the disposal of the Ottomans, whose aim was self-satisfaction through a narrow maximization of taxation and military state system along ethno-religious lines. Among others, the *devşirme* tax (also known as the "blood tax"), was a heart-breaking price to pay for non-Muslim families who were not excluded according to ethnic belonging. It is clear that while Ottoman toleration towards plural confessional laws allowed regulation of personal and collective cases within each Millet, Orthodox Patriarchs remained subaltern in front of the Sultan. Similarly, taxation management was entrusted to the *sipâhi* (e.g., Ottoman cavalry corps) and the *zaim* (e.g., military governor of the land tenure of Empire), both appointed by the dominant group because of cultural belonging (Fukuyama 2011).

In contemporary liberal democracies, Kymlicka's attempt to soften clashes within diverse "societal cultures" are prompt to fail on the ground because of his approach to a past model of toleration, such as the Millet-style system mentioned above. Although Kymlicka philosophically distances himself from such a model of toleration by stressing his agreement with John Rawls's political liberalism. However, Kymlicka's list of national minorities, immigrant groups, and others shows the same problem of his positive model for religious toleration. For instance, the assumption that immigrant minorities will always have less readiness than "nation-people" to integrate themselves into the larger society does not grip on the ground. Recently, the increase of societal ties between Muslim members of national minorities and new-coming immigrant groups are strengthening, and thereby showing the opposite. Also, such a distinction theoretically does not follow any normative approach, thereby remaining highly controversial for the neutral role of the State which should respect and stand for specific-minority rights and (for example) deny them for security purposes. Without any doubts, this affects performativity of toleration and misleads the principle of tolerance itself. Similarly, the Millet-style model of religious toleration, liberal democracies today promote tolerance on the surface of the realm without, as a matter of fact, enforcing everyday practices of tolerance. According to Gramsci, today's performativity of tolerance has to take root if and only if the ideological state apparatus can benefit from certain ways of "equally" recognising and "tolerating" the (subaltern) Others without eroding or impinging on the majoritarian cultural system's set of religious beliefs, education, and traditional values. In other words, liberal institutions support and allow a model of toleration along with a notion of tolerance as long as they can avoid (trans-)/formation that hegemonic power structures might culturally face and need to tackle politically. In this sense, intersectional aspects of gender, ethnic, or racial issues are instructive of how traditional democracies are far from granting recognition even to those worthwhile practices or sets of beliefs that might trigger transformation in the civil society. However, this liberal model of recognising and allocating specific group rights into the larger society is not far from leftist attempts whose theoretical approach grants a full integration of subaltern into "one and indivisible people" without recognizing differences from within.

In order to conclude this section, what could be understood through the prism of the "paradox of tolerance," it is only one of the large number of paradoxes that affect our contemporary societies in a time of deep crisis which (cyclically) lasts for decades, just as Gramsci had noticed in what he called "organic crisis." This time of ongoing crisis began in the post-1989 era when other Western philosophers had (mistakenly) proclaimed the "end of history." By paraphrasing Gramsci (op. cit. 178), the "tolerance paradox" of our time results from the exceptional duration of such time of crisis, which is incurable and shows the fractures of the structural conditions on which our society is based. These structural conditions of contemporary democracies have already revealed themselves even though only political forces—namely, current populist élites—express willingness to conserve and defend in order to cure them, therefore to maintain their positions. Looking beneath the surface of lack of tolerance in the light of cultural differences among a population means to understand how certain notions of tolerance and solidarity are allowed rather than others. If the firsts are permitted through a superficial, or highly ideological approach of liberal humanitarianism, the seconds may (not) indicate a more accurate model of toleration, which would help to better convey a wider, epistemologically accurate, time-sensitive, and locally nuanced picture of power dynamics without overlooking different characteristics within and between social groups at the same time.

CHAPTER NINE

Gramscianism: Marxism Otherwise?

In the previous chapters, a philosophical ground, perhaps slightly revisionist, has been set up for analysing Gramsci's contribution to a wealth of minority issues in general and the (in-)tolerance issue in particular.

Following Gramsci's (slippery) terminology, it seems that both political and cultural circumstances of subaltern groups have utterly failed because they have not been properly addressed and formulated. For the large majority of cases, so-called "multiculturalism", particularly "multicultural cosmopolitanism", has encountered the old paradox of "cultural identity". In general, the more time and effort that is spent over subaltern communities to pave the way, or establish the roadmap, for a "way out" from subalternity as well as marginality, the more multiculturalists paradoxically employ an array of ethnic, racial, indigenous, or sexual features of identity that they culturally fight to let them be included in the "core society". This paradoxical, subaltern conditionality of minority groups has been described by Slavoj Žižek in the last few years. His position here, as he himself admitted, is reminiscent of the issue that Frédéric Lordon, French social theorist and critical thinker, touches upon while demonstrating how the cosmopolitan anti-nationalist intellectualism advocating "liberation from belonging" tends, in extremis, to dismiss every search for roots and every attachment to a particular ethnic or cultural identity as an almost proto-fascist stance (2017: 206). Similarly, multiculturalism in all its nuances has been accused of being nothing more than another form of communitarianism, whose approach lies subtly in the gentle and open-minded theory of recognition of cultural differences within a social realm is nothing but a veiled-led form of essentialist community that multiculturalism itself aims to contrast.

In fact, post-Communist subaltern groups' positionality sheds light on nothing but today's post-Communist Europe lasting "organic crisis", too premature to be defined as concluded. Although democratic transition of CEE has moved on for three decades after the geopolitical "1989 earthquake", the poor achievement of full-fledged democracy standards has come to show how such transition is still ongoing and far from being defined as accomplished. While much emphasis has been put on the process of transition (e.g., transformation of policies, institutions, the rule of law), little attention has been paid to people's "culture of everyday life of civility" (Havel 1996: 29). With regards to the role of minority groups, indeed, tendency toward cultural marginalisation and ethno-nationalist centrism has shown that there is still a long way to go. Therefore, the historical paradigm of the "organic crisis" could be understood as a chance for subaltern groups to get acquainted with their past experiences and disentangle the linchpins of instrumental fabrications of marginalisation and exclusion throughout those societies in which they have been and continue to live while being set apart.

In addition, Gramsci's uncanny insights give a different angle of investigation than that of the "struggle of recognition" or the non-mediated class action for the dissolution of the society. According to the subject-matter of this study, a few, albeit relevant, human conditions have to be addressed through Gramsci's use of the term "subaltern". The latter would play a vital role in readdressing major concerns in CEE contemporary democracies. Whether the uncommon use of the term "*ceto*" rather than "class" owns a philosophical relevancy if juxtaposed with the largely used Marxist orthodox "class struggle", the internal division among different segments of subaltern groups is here important to reinterpret the human condition of subalternity as habit of being resulting from externally imposed ascription. For example, if compared to the Theory of Minority Rights (Kymlicka 1995), or the Politics of Recognition (Taylor 2004), or Fukuyama's End of History (1992), Gramsci's "Theory of Hegemony" displays how power structures of exclusion are more than just "ethnic" or "religious" or "cultural" and so forth. In fact, while the post-Communist "ethnic democracy" (Krasniqi 2010: 523) was imposed through a modelling form of othering based on the majoritarian ethnos that had become the only permissible group-forming entity, today's minority groups show how subaltern political or cultural status contains hegemonic and non-hegemonic in itself. With regard to the above-mentioned Habermas's and Fraser's models of public spheres, hegemony's structures of exclusion have to be investigated from within minority actorness in order to deconstruct internally multi-layered entities and shed light on the so-called subaltern counter-publics. Within these, indeed, opinions and claims have to be realigned in the course of discourse, providing a space of existence for leading an emergence and development of common narratives, identities, and capacities for collective actions (Német and Rézműves 2018: 50) prior to setting up a space of self-governing or representation.

In this regard, realignment of the voiceless position of women, disabled, LGBTQI+, paperless, and so forth, means to adjust the asymmetries created by dominant discourse and its parallel dominated one. It means, in other words, to realign a fairly confrontational asymmetry that directly results from the dualism that hegemony creates through the imposed actorness of the State and of the civil society.

In turn, a Gramscian perspective becomes here centrally paramount for understanding a new nuance of the confrontational binarism between the State and the civil society. In fact, Gramsci's category of (non-)hegemonic domination does not only display political-cultural as well as ethical-moral asymmetry between the domination State, which speaks both the language and the culture of its epoch by interrupting subaltern voices from the civil society. It also displays the asymmetrical positionality within the State itself — namely, between the existing ruling élites over traditional intellectuals, and the civil society's actorness. This picture, which for Laclau denotes an ambiguous facet of Gramsci's vis-à-vis State/civil society opposition, should refer to a poststructuralist (e.g., post-modern) approach in the attempt to disentangle inconspicuous, albeit present, subaltern minority issues currently existing from within an already-recognised and instrumentally allowed subaltern communities. In this, overlooking the normative paradigm means neither to dismiss nor to undermine already-made studies on the "post"-Communist public sphere in the region. Rather, in the Gramscian sense, it would eventually mean to give credit to a (colonial) notion of subalternity, useful to deepen the status of minorityhood and how the latter — which as identified in terms of counter-publics — encompasses subaltern positions from within. This is why legal recognition and public accreditation of cultural claims, needs, and requests of subaltern groups within an already-dominated community (counter-public) have not yet been recognised by the public as well as by the counter-public's actorness composed of those minority ruling voices that are allowed to confront the public's in the arena of discourse. If we confront such perspective with the example of legal recognition of minority rights, we would clearly figure out and be aware of how the latter represents only an extension of conditional parameters to fulfil the State's transition towards a full-fledged democracy. Under the parapet of such "full recognition", Gramsci would point out how the latter is nothing else than a cultural and political manifestation of asymmetrical forces of ruling and existing leadership. Similar to the case of "(in-)tolerance paradox", such recognition is nothing but a perpetuation of the hegemonic imposition of certain recognition. In a few words, an instrumental recognition. Phenomena described so far, such as "positive discrimination" (Laclau and Mouffe 1994) and post-Communist (post-colonial) positionality of subalterns, are just instructive.

Moreover, Gramsci's category of hegemony may open yet another "revisionist" chapter of his philosophical contribution to Marxism. In insights, Southeast European subaltern groups have negotiable principles by which they struggle for their recognition and improvement of everyday condition. For Gramsci, this aspect does not concern a major problem at all among those subjected to a status of subalternity. In fact, "subaltern classes" cannot be reduced into a vis-à-vis antagonism against hegemonic forces, but they—through the role of organic intellectuals at first—have to lead a movement determined in, and capable of, producing history as a new narrative of truth. This results from what Gramsci's extension to the issue of class-position/class-consciousness through the prism of cultural and political role of intellectuals describes as into the hegemony (Spivak 1999: 269).

By attempting to follow the Gramscian tradition of subaltern, "subalternity" is nothing but a literally Medieval Latin-oriented reference to "sub", namely "below", and "altern", namely "alter", or, more precisely, "of other", understood in the philosophical dialectical movement of "*alterare*" — namely "to make alter" from "below". The prefix "sub" points not only out those people outside the majoritarian cultural system but also the subaltern community beneath it. As a matter of fact, this might be one of the most relevant insights of Gramsci's contribution. Coming into dominance for leading to a new hegemony in order to replace the former one, changes completely the angle of the investigation so far used by Marxist scholarship. The idea that subaltern groups have to lead themselves into hegemony by including some elements of hegemonic forces and replacing them, thereby becoming dominant in turn, and overthrowing its own status of nonhegemonic positionality and subalternity, is centrally paramount for the establishment of new literature. Along with a contribution "from below", Gramsci's legacy definitely highlights more inconspicuous, albeit vivid and present, cultural facets of subalternity (e.g., different sexual orientation, liberal views within religious groups, anti-patriarchal discourse) and hidden issues within the subaltern minority groups (e.g., peasantry, paperless migrants, minorities-within-a minority).

Although Gramsci is recognised as one of the first fathers of the so-called "radical democracy", one of antagonistic positions in struggle toward domination, such prospective inclusion of hegemonic models of ruling and existing hegemony by subaltern communities is a turning-point for the entire Marxist tradition in social science. While the hegemony displays structures of instrumental exclusion, the latter underpins the dialectical power of subaltern position and further opportunity to lead a replacement of hegemony itself. In fact, Gramsci's category of hegemony is practically contingent and philosophically teleological. The latter, indeed, owns in itself a potential trajectory leading a direction in social life. In other words, hegemony is a hidden movement to activate in so far as a potential desire is claimed from below, which consciously confronts the already-existing hegemony in the attempt to replace it. Because of this, intellectual recognition of subaltern knowledge has to come first into a new space of existence and discourse. Such recognition, which Gramsci refers to in terms of recognisability (see Open Conclusions), can happen not only on a normative ground, but also on a cultural one. Particularly interesting for a Marxist thinker, elements of literature and art are understood by the Sardinian philosopher Gramsci as instruments of (re)cognisability. This dissociates Gramsci himself from the critically orthodox "vulgar Marxism", whose philosophical consideration of both Art and Literature was reduced to the idea that these two elements result directly from the ruling ideology, namely – from those expressions and conditions that the "common sense" hierarchically imposes by the ideology in the society social beings are born in. Or, conversely, two ways of expression that constitute a dilemma regarding the effects on sociality in the same work of art and artistic production. Here, Gramsci came along the Marxist criticism that treats Literature and Art as a special area within (or even adjacent to) ideology. However, a work of art reveals a leading force that constitutes a kind of artistic partisanship aimed at intensifying the clarity, the distinctness and the whole objectivity of what the same work of art is arranging and ordering through the attempt of the artist (e.g., the maker of art) to spring out the quality of reality into practices against the aesthetic illusion of what the bourgeoisie imposes. However, although Friedrich Engels, and Vladimir Lenin after him, argues about a certain tendentiousness of a work of art, the latter, only if cognised, possesses an ability to reflect upon ideological conflicts of a historical period. It would be possible within this critical tradition to talk about literature as having a relative autonomy, and placing Gramsci ahead of orthodox Marxists, who had never formulated a sociology of art and whose only incidental discussion on Art in general, or Literature in particular, reflected a wide range of aesthetics, political and economic issues (Selden 1990: 63-64, 402, 442).

To conclude, the subject-matter of this study may shed a new kind of light over the recognition of minority cultures and micro-histories. As Noam Chomsky noticed, after a time of uncertainty and disorder, where cruelty and violence has taken place, an inspection of the published record (e.g. reviews, books, articles in major intellectual journals) can be extremely instructive (1999: 40). Recognisability is first and foremost existential rather than exclusively normative or political. It is aimed at potentially leading everyone toward a hegemonic dominancy which guarantees access to a circle of humanity, where the old paradox regarding the fact that more marginalisation and exclusion seems to allow groups or individuals to assert more exclusive ways of life, is avoidable. In fact, what Gramsci seems to emphasise is the importance of practising reverence without idealisation: remembering that every being is an intellectual, without casting upon them projections of nonmediated revolution or dismissal of the society they live in.

OPEN CONCLUSIONS

"I have been amazed by the can-do philosophy and the nonchalance with which certain policy planners invent their own solution models without asking whether the antagonists will ever be willing or able to implement them."

Geert-Hinrich Ahrens (2007)

"We, the froth at the top of it,
were celebrating the triumph of freedom
and openness and plurality and fantasy
and pleasure and all of that.
That was frivolous,
and I am deeply ashamed."

Gáspár Miklós Tamás (2009)

CHAPTER TEN
In Search of a New Praxis

Throughout the progression of post-Communist CEE to a wealthier and more desirable region of full-fledged democracies, themes and issues of multiculturalism and pluralism have been scholarly fascinating. Three decades onward, the apparent failure of their proposals has brought the early figures and promoters who had pioneered multiculturalism and pluralistic society to leave the room of discussion. Because of this, the main purpose of this monograph was to turn such pessimist scenery into a different path left largely untraveled by the majority of critical thinkers and other scholars. Worth reconsidering a pessimism in intellect and an optimism of the well – according to Gramsci, trying however to avoid too trivial interpretation no matter how depressing the situation is (Marchart 2018:209).

For better and not worse, Gramsci's work and legacy of critical studies have been used as the central perspective through which trying to reorient the philosophical enquiry on minority groups. Within the contested and turbulent space of the former Eastern Bloc, the attempt to go backward the trajectory of the Gramscian scholarship, from Spivak's critical question "Can Subaltern Speak?" (1988) to the same Sardinian "curious" contribution in Marxism, aimed at introducing a new kind of philosophical paradigm for looking beneath minority issues and thereby shifting the subject of discussion to a confrontational terrain of discussion. Aware of many other qualified scholars that have so far worked hard on potential applications of Gramsci's philosophy of praxis in academia and beyond, this monograph aims to draw a few remarkably suggestive insights related to the almost untranslatable Gramscian terminology in order to rethink key aspects of subaltern groups in general, and interconnectedness of domination and subordination in particular.

To begin with, the strong criticism of interdisciplinary methodologies has been directed to their continuous attempt to largely frame the societal actorness of minority groups through static and one-dimensional categorisation. As previously stated, the fact is that the term "minority" has been reduced to a mere term of simplistic description that barely suits the real state of affairs of a given minority group in its contingency. The term itself, which was extremely useful in the aftermaths of the Second World War, silences the various layers of a given collective, thereby showing its fallacious nature through a wrong action of inverting, and often confusing, causes and effects of "minorityhood". "Gypsyism"[1], among others, one of the latest newly-coined terms and field of study, displays partially the large number of instances related to how Roma integration has failed. By considering both de-politicisation and de-mobilisation of Roma groups as a consequence of their lack of capability rather than investigating the role of political representatives and subtle ways of selecting and electing leaders, there is still a pious hope that their micro-political space of neglected existences could be democratically represented in a forum of rational and valid debate. Moreover, the idea to narrow down a specific bunch of people to a rigid framework of cultural features is nothing but an externally imposed act of naming, that is, an act of possessing certain segments of society, which overlooks and undermines the multi-layered and intersectional complexity of intra-group dynamics. Hence, criticism toward both conceptualisation of "minority" as a term, and "cultural identity" as a scholarly paradigm along "ethnic" lines, has been employed to pinpoint today's irrelevancy of the term "ethnos" as "a people", which is never the case.

In this regard, the term "subaltern" in Gramsci's sense, rather than "minority", has been introduced to better pursue a critical analysis of the issues at stake, thereby challenging the discourse of "ethno-politics" and its tendency to employ static and monolithic paradigms for identifying the societal role of cultures and identities. Again aware of the volatility, vagueness, riskiness, and perhaps outrageousness in some cases of the term "minority", this monograph should have avoided such pitfall by using a Gramscian perspective.

Thus, as the title suggests, the term "subalternity" attempts to introduce the paradigm of "subalternity" not only as a thematic instrument to deal with, but also for tackling the difficulty of assimilating Gramsci's sociological insights and making the contemporary discussion over the minority issues clearer. It also contains the teleological challenge to deal with "subalternity" as a new paradigmatic term to employ integrally in policy plans, reference papers, deliberative strategies, and so forth. In turn, the decision to replace "minority" with "subaltern" has

---

[1] See more Antigypsyism – A Reference Paper, Version June 2017, European Roma Grassroots Organizations (ERGO) Network and Central Council of German Sinti and Roma (last accessed 15/07/2019 from www.antigypsyism.eu)

nothing to do with an academia-oriented attitude to introduce a new niche to be used as justification for this study. In front of the delicate operation of assigning a "name" for identifying a collective being, which remains a crucial decision reflected on a political level, the attempt of de-grounding and regrounding such terrain of investigation is aimed at revitalising a polemical critique rather than indulging in the narcissism of minor differences into today's struggle-like academic competition. Following Laclau's Political Theory of Naming (Marchart 2018: 161-180), naming is grounding and preempting externally imposed ascriptions. Thus, the introduction of subalternity as a new paradigmatic term has been aimed at digging deeply into both human conditionality of marginal existence and externally imposed ascription of cultural patronisation upon certain cultures and communities. In fact, the digging angle of investigation that subalternity offers sheds light at the same time on neglected human condition existing, yet overlooked or kept at check, within intra-group minority dynamics and stemming from the language of the everyday life. In other words, replacing the term "minority" with "subaltern" means to disentangle those instrumentally excluded and traditionally marginalised segments of society from the constant exposition to the malignant construction of Otherness. In this regard, subalternity could be extremely useful for navigating within and in between the different voices seeking recognition from within subaltern entities they are part of and belong to. By doing so, pre-empting the pitfall that sociology and anthropology continue to fall into while using the term "minority" and thereby ascribing certain feature upon a societal group, is of central relevancy. At the same time, "subaltern" is a complementary, paradigmatic term for being more attentive to the hidden proximity of different internal voices. In the case of Muslim minority groups, for example, subalternity can disentangle the mechanism that renders women's and LGBTQI+'s claims of cultural rights voiceless by internal members of the same minority group, and by an antiMuslim discourse (e.g., Islamophobia) tending to generalise the multifaceted and intersectional phenomena of Islam into a fundamentalist religion intolerant and deaf toward the same women's and LGBTQI+'s rights.

Hence, the Gramscian track of "subaltern groups" and his critique against a patronising discourse of the "working class" as quintessence of the Great Proletariat upon subaltern peasantry, re-examines subalternity not only with regard to old-fashioned issues of minority groups (e.g., national minorities, indigenous peoples, Roma groups). It does also upon the large number of newly-arrived issues seeking out recognition within the minority they are formulated in. Indeed, Nancy Fraser's reference to "subaltern counter-publics" (1992) labels such unheard voices, which are rendered subaltern in respect to separate counter-publics functioning in dialectical opposition to the publics. In the Habermas's public sphere model, the counterpublics aim to check-and-balance the discourse in the public sphere through a rational discourse. Nevertheless, they often fail to address messages from the subaltern counter-publics and convey them. To put it simply, counterpublics are the result of the ideological manipulation of publics' discourse, which is, in Gramsci's terms, the one of the State that speaks the languages of its epoch. In this regard, State's most powerful form of possessing is naming subaltern groups and their (sub-)cultures through which a certain set of prescribing and ascribing features are imposed in order to dismantle their leading potential toward the universal. This is what the State does through imposing a "proper" name, which is nothing else than a projection of possession based on knowledge exploitation.

What might here seem to be another conundrum of the deliberative democracy, against which raising the question of what form of social struggle might subaltern undertake, it might instead be easily at least discovered by using the Gramscian (slippery) terminology.

In this regard, a move forward requires once again a few disclaimers.

To begin with, although "subaltern" has increased academic recognition as a scholarly term, there is yet no use of it, or its philosophical nature and social implications, among minority policy planners, special rapporteurs, or minority advocates. In general, "subaltern" has been almost exclusively used in the academic circle in its adjective form in the attempt to replace more common terms such as "oppressed", "enslaved", and so forth. With respect to the former Eastern Bloc's minority issues, the use of "subaltern" may thus sound naïve. From this viewpoint, disagreement on interpreting certain minority affairs, or naming specific communities, in terms of "oppressed" or "enslaved" and so forth, may arise. However, after all, CEE countries—with a few exceptions[2], of course—have ratified and domestically adopted international conventions and public policies in defence of minority groups and recognition of their cultural rights. Terms such as "oppression" or "slavery" or "serf" do not really depict the variety of minority issues. After having sketched many examples

---

[2] The much-discussed "Istanbul Convention", one of the Council of Europe's most recent conventions, aimed at combatting violence against women and domestic violence, has not been ratified and was stopped from coming into force by almost all post-Communist European Nations: Armenia, Azerbaijan, Bulgaria, Czech Republic, Hungary, Latvia, Lithuania, Moldovia, Slovakia, and Ukraine. See more: https://www.coe.int/en/web/conventions/full-list//conventions/treaty/210/signatures

related to minority groups across the region, key characteristics are the intersectional and multi-layered myriad of societal manifestations that the use of "subalternity" may undertake.

In the second part of the monograph, "subalternity" stands out as a reflective angle of investigation of minorityhood, which is nothing but a human condition of marginalisation and instrumental exclusion prior to be considered a form of political subordination. This is why, from an epistemological viewpoint, the term "subaltern" in replacement of "minority" has to be understood in accordance with its literally Medieval Latin origin. As introduced, here subaltern stands for: "sub-", namely "below", and "-altern", namely "alter", or, more precisely, "of an Other". This paradigmatic term, which is clearly twofold, refer to the philosophical dialectical movement of *"alterare"* — namely "to make alter" — from "below". Therefore, the prefix "sub-" may not only point out subaltern people outside the majoritarian cultural system, but also those bunches of peoples who are unheard, voiceless, and hidden within the society they belong to.

This different, and epistemologically relevant insight gears toward two philosophically crucial implications.

First of all, the proposal of the "subalternity paradigm" does not only tackle the patronising and colonising act of identifying minority groups with regard to their cultures in general, or behavioural patterns and ethnic features in particular. It does not meanwhile take for granted the sometimes herculean attempt to navigate in between and across the paradoxes that minority issues are composed of, and oftentimes trapped in. Because of this, "subalternity" also avoids vernacular politicisation of too-culturalist differentiation of groups, which ignores externally imposed stigmatising mechanisms upon certain minority cultures and identities. In a few words, the use of the term "subaltern" contains the practical aim to critically question the power linchpins from which marginalisation is born and around which it is instrumentally created and maintained as such.

It followed that Jacques Derrida's "de-constructivism" represents a potential method of reading onto the construction of the politicality and critically disentangling political discourses ascribed to a given collective identity. Along with it, the introduction of the paradigm of subalternity is not only used for better highlighting the causes of a large number of minority issues to deal properly with. Following once again Ernesto Laclau's "Political Theory of Naming", subalternity serves as a name to be introduced in the attempt to de-ground the subject of discussion and disentangle it from those prescriptive nodal points that hegemons impose to possess the totality of a given chain.

Thereby, a Gramscian use of the term "subaltern" has to be taken into account for a better and deeper enquiry of today's societal hierarchies, particularly for pre-empting externally ascribed features imposed upon a unity and thereby highlighting the origins of relations of subordination and possession.

According to the increasing criticism against multiculturalism, for instance, Etiene Balibar argues that a contemporary form of "meta-racism" has won the ground because of implementations of multicultural policies that postulate nothing but a legitimate presence of a "superior tolerator" and a patronised different Other to be tolerated. Subtly, "identity politics" has taken over such contradiction of multicultural societies and is used as the simplest and most logical expansion of a new kind of racism against those who are supposed to tolerate. In other words, attempts to accommodate cultural differences have instead come to legitimize diversity insofar as the latter remains as such. This has thus reinforced ideas that "minorities have got special privileges" (Castellino 2018: 350), thereby spreading out a further conviction related to the fact that multiculturalism "has gone too far" (Murray 2018: 94).

In this instance, a major concern with this exclusively implicit and subtler attitude of multicultural policies aiming genuinely at avoiding conflicts and pacifying tensions, has been pointed out. It seems indeed that implementations of multicultural policies have done nothing but perpetuate cultural divisions among social groups of peoples by trying to accommodate differences into cultural and political agencies. From the "minority perspective", one may agree on the fact that multiculturalism is understood as a form of veiled "liberal nationalism", such as Kymlicka's. Looking beneath the contemporary phenomena of vernacularism and discriminatory, multiculturalism has paradoxically set up the terrain for banal representation of identities and simplistic representation of cultures (König 2002: 51). In fact, a certain "façade parity" has never been guaranteed if peoples and cultures are not depicted as different from each other and reduced to their cultural features (e.g., ethnicity, race, class, gender, nationality), and without which they could not seek and achieve recognition or being recognised (Gáspár Miklós Tamás 2019). In this case, liberal models of multiculturalism and its performativity model of public policies are deeply rooted in conservative forces (Raud 2016: 383) that reinforce features of differences, which should be instead addressed confrontationally in order to guarantee recognition to any individual and/or any specific group at risk. Unsurprisingly, Zygmunt Bauman stood against the principles that multiculturalism is based on, because multiculturalism itself has been acting just like racism before it and passing in silence the fact that social inequality is a vastly self-fulfilling phenomenon and that representation of multiplying social divisions born of inequality is the inevitable product of free choice (Bauman 2001: 48, cited by Raud 2016: 383).

Granted that asserting the identity of marginalised and oppressed segments or groups of society does not equal asserting inequalities in Western nations and their societies, imposed victimhood upon subalterns of any kind cannot longer represent a certain Western proposal of multicultural society. The latter is indeed composed of a subtler, perhaps implicit, reconfiguration of unjust forms of colonisation that perpetrate a "positive discrimination" through the moral superiority of a "tolerator". Although a post-colonial paradigm may be useful to dig into, and look beneath, contested pages of history and power fabrication of subordination, there is the need to shed new light on inconspicuous, albeit vivid, struggles of minority groups rejecting the idea of being "the Other", which robs their political identities that hegemons have imposed upon them and rule over (Žižek 2017: 179–224).

Against this pitfall, the purpose of the introduction of the paradigmatic term "subalternity" aims to shift the accusation towards multiculturalism as a whole onto a different path. To a certain extent, multiculturalism does not foresee a priori divisions in society, at least in theory. Instead, if multiculturalism has to be accused of reinforcing divisions and inequality, a philosophical investigation has to look at policy implementations and particularly the interlink with power asymmetries produced instrumentally throughout the society. So far, if multiculturalism has utterly failed to provide a fair space of coexistence and shape a collective desire to live together, the origin of such failure cannot be found in multiculturalism in itself, but rather in the nature of power structures and the instrumental divisions that cultural hierarchies impose throughout "our" contemporary democracy. In this regard, a certain overwhelming attitude of pathologising (liberal) multiculturalism in its theoretical (perhaps ideological?) facets, which recalls the paradigmatic term "subalternity" rather than "minority" or "minorityhood", is confusing causes and effects of certain minority issues".

Above all, indeed, "subalternity" avoids here an essentialisation of minority cultures and their identities, which currently leaves room for a form of "postmodern racism" (mentioned by Salecl 1994: 11). Although it does not function as the older form of discrimination, such form of racism subtly reimposes culturally hierarchized structures which do not allow certain values and norms due to the specific segments of cultural, social, and political groups that seek them out with the attempt to legitimise them.

In other words, offering a replacement of the term "minority" with "subaltern" means to aim at better identifying those inconspicuous struggles of the needy, the marginalised, and the excluded subaltern groups by avoiding the assumptions to understand these societal groups and their cultures—no matter if from the social majority or minority—as essentially static (Hasan 2010: 61) and internally homogenous. What may look like only a scholarly replacement may facilitate digging into multi-layered aspects of a given subaltern group and recognising the different subaltern voices within an already-dominated group. In turn, a refusal of the one-dimensional taxonomy of peoplehood will mean to critically reject certain "too culturalist" and "primordialist" sources perpetuating the projection of banal assumptions of lack of skills, biological inferiority, cultural relativisms, and substandard education, to name a few. This is centrally paramount to disrupt the practical function of (liberal) multiculturalism to impose certain ascription upon societal groups whose genuine justifications are aimed at recognising disadvantageous positions in society, yet produce the subtler contrary effect of reinforcing stereotypes of inferiority and hopelessness.

After all, both politicisation and cosmopolitan theories for minority rights (see Will Kymlicka 1992) have become nowadays highly problematic on the ground. Lack of capacity in addressing legally multifaceted complex compositions of any subaltern group on the one hand, and "façade recognition" on the other hand, overlook a large number of intra-group dynamics (e.g., "internal extroverts", individual positions, potential "exit strategies", private issues), whose issues cannot be posited in the hands of a contemporary liberal (neutral) State. Incapable of intervening for accommodating claims and needs, the liberal State seems deaf to certain yells that speak up against political discrimination and cultural exclusion.

Second of all, the introduction of subalternity requires here a properly philosophical disclaimer regarding the burning question of "hegemony". As largely sketched in the second part of this monograph, Gramsci's notion of hegemony is extremely subtle in its functions and philosophically sophisticated to grasp. This difficulty to correctly understand Gramsci's Theory of Hegemony results from a philosophical tendency to frame the Sardinian philosopher's philosophy of praxis in consequence of Marx's analysis of society. This is not exactly the case indeed. For example, in Gramsci's sense, both cultural and political functions of hegemony coming violently into existence do not literally refer to an ideological position under which exploitation, pain, anger, and sorrow are suffered. Of course, from a historical point of view minorities have been exposed to, and went through, diverse experiences of violent and cruel actions which have threatened their existence. Yet, on a philosophical ground, Gramsci went beyond Marx in developing a theory of ideology which acted at the level of superstructure rather than the economic base. Therefore, if one really wants to follow a Gramscian understanding of how hegemony grips throughout society, s/he has to consider hegemony itself as a mere "perspective of opportunities". By borrowing such approach, hegemony becomes the breach through which looking closely at the power structures and discovering the opportunities within which both cultural and political opportunities might be found to move (potentially) ahead.

In fact, following Gramsci, hegemony requires a certain framework of participation, which must begin with an enjoyment of the elements of hegemony. In practice, perhaps too political, here the question is not how to propose a non-mediated destructive action against "hegemony" as a strategy that most probably the majority of orthodox Marxists would agree on. From a philosophical viewpoint, Gramsci's language recalls the Hegelian metaphor of "Mastery and Servitude" in the "*Phenomenology of Spirit*" (1807). In fact, Gramsci seems to have conceptualised the Theory of Hegemony by knowing the reciprocal and mutual relation between two poles of mediations understood as two major super-structural levels: the (hegemonic) Masterhood or mastery, which is the result of the overwhelming coercion and dominant consent that divides and rules over the subalterns, the servants, who are governed by it. Therefore, Gramsci's concept of hegemony is neither negative nor exclusively picture an image of oppression, colonial slavery, and restless struggle against institutions to be defeated. On the contrary, hegemony is potentially a perspective of opportunities through which a teleological reparation and recognition can be achieved (Hovhannisyan and Mkrtchyan 2016: 110–119).

In this regard, the proposed adjective "teleological", from the Greek "telos" (τέλος), which literally means "purpose" or "scope", is not used randomly here. In fact, "hegemony" is here undertaken by partially refusing Marx's "liberation struggle" which, unlike Gramsci, essentialises hegemony and frames it into a reductive dichotomy of "bourgeoisie oppression" upon the "working classes" whose lack of unity disempowers subalterns to embody a class for-itself—namely, a conscious entity able to become a collective political actor.

Nowadays, hegemonic political and cultural power structures patronise subtly and implicitly minority groups through a colonial-like action of dispossession and dismissal of certain minority knowledge and cultural features at the expense of the dominant majority's. As explained in Part One, the term "colonial" has to be found in the long-term trajectory of post-colonial studies, yet in terms of "coloniality of being". Once again, there is a lot of distance with the term decolonisation and decolonial, which, once again, remain political projects where violence is always present (Fanon 2001: 27). Hence, one may affirm that (post-)coloniality is a newly liberal multicultural form of political thinking and cultural knowing that has emerged through externally constructed boundaries based on interests of hegemons (Castellino 2018: 344) working on a cultural level at first, and in turn on the political level, at second. In turn, it is extremely important to understand that this coloniality shifts gears in relation to "ethnic", "gender", "radical", and, to a certain extent, "political" features of already-dominated groups, within which certain segments are rendered subaltern. In other words, hegemonic forces generally function by negating, disavowing, distorting, and denying equal parity to different forms of certain knowledge and life visions which compose societal groups. By doing so, hegemony particularly sets certain values and norms aside in order to prepare the terrain for the emerging (historical) bloc to come to power and impose its own cultural and political direction in social life and people's everydayness.

After all, indeed, Gramsci's reference to "hegemony" in terms of *direzione*—namely, from the Italian language, is here used to organise subalterns toward a complete disruption of their positionality by thereby leading them toward a new existence in a new hegemonic position where circumstances of "inferiority", "secondary", "being tolerated", and so forth, do not play any role whatsoever. In order to do so, the Gramscian desire sees the creation of hegemonic condition of former subalterns through cultural institutions and autonomous devices like factory councils, self-organised spaces, and political subjects prompt to action. To a certain extent, it gives priority to a designed roadmap that underlines how the disruption of the human condition of subalternity has to prepare, and be prepared in, the terrain of confrontational discourse that empowers all those left behind.

To begin with, participation—or "enjoyment of elements of hegemony"—means to be awakened from a colonised human condition and to start formulating a discourse for gaining consensus among subalterns. In addition, as Gramsci pointed out, participation means nothing but becoming aware of subalternity in itself and for itself, namely, a leading action towards a conscious and complete disruption of the subaltern (colonised) human condition. This is yet another difference between the use of the term "subaltern" in the de-colonial discourse and the "subaltern paradigm" in this study. While the former remains largely a political option against the status quo, the latter sheds light on a possible new perspective for looking beneath the status quo. The introduction of the "subaltern paradigm" is thus a momentous step in the struggle for recognition, one which does not need to focus on normative aspects of minority issues and deal with them, taking the risk of pathologising the issues at stake. Above all, Gramsci's "participation" inside the hegemonic structure of political and cultural dominant is aimed at destabilising the productive mechanism of subalternity and its historicalpolitical nature and origins.

Granted that subalternity would be used to acknowledge certain human (colonised) conditions with their widely varying forms of existence and intensities of potential leading actorness, the proposal for a roadmap becomes here problematic, yet worth trying to introduce.

While hegemonised human conditions of certain subaltern groups can be easily replaced through the creation of a new kind of socio-political direction leading toward a new hegemony to construct and impose in social life, politicisation and mobilisation of intellectuals within the minority have to be organised. Against what Laclau suggests to move from a conception of traditional to organic intellectuals, this study has focussed more on the societal actorness of the traditional rather than the organic intellectuals. At the same time, however, it must be pointed out that Gramsci found very difficult to completely exorcise the Marxist concept of so-called "false consciousness" (Lears 1985: 578). While the Sardinian philosopher moved away from such "false consciousness", emphasising the autonomy of ideology and its primary moment in history (e.g., "organic crisis"), his introduction of a "contradictory consciousness" composed of apathy, sometimes resistance, or even resignation among subalterns, remains only an alternative to Marx's. Perhaps, what Gramsci referred to as "contradictory consciousness" was a weak remedy to substitute Marx's standpoint over the production of ideology of the bourgeoisie upon subaltern classes, on the one hand, and the consequential "false consciousness" in the social life, on the other hand. Hence, both paradigms and "types of consciousness" are not about the impossibility to awake subaltern groups in their sociality. Rather, it must be about a negative possession of identity, namely, an accepted consciousness that minority groups possess with knowledge and consciousness despite the fact it reflects a subaltern status. Paraphrasing Gramsci, such negative possession of identity seems to confirm a political apathy of certain contested minority groups considered "culturally inferior" to the majority identity", such as that of Aromanians in the Balkans, or Pomaks in Bulgaria; the resistance of feminist groups, LGBTQI+ community, and secular voices within traditional Muslim groups; or even the resignation of ample segments of Roma populations who think of themselves as "vote sellers" are just three instructive cases of such "negative possession of subaltern identity". Even more frankly, a large number of minority issues stem from suspicious behavioural patterns that minority groups are consciously responsible for and which they get something out of. This might be understood as the real Achilles's heel of policy implementation aimed at mobilising minority groups. According to the former Eastern Bloc, for example, the risk of allocating a large degree of territorial autonomy or selfgoverning rights to a federalist system is that it would potentially endorse breakaway entities and impinge on State integrity; or, a full recognition of cultural or religious rights would begin to trigger processes of ghettoisation of ethnic or religious clusters of people into neighbourhoods or specific regions, and facilitate further phenomena of radicalisation or disloyalty toward the State institutions.

Because of this, this current monograph has (re)introduced the relevant topics of traditional intellectuals and organic intellectuals in Gramsci's analysis of society. Rather than the latter, in fact, who tend to fail to convey and represent all voices of the group they speak on behalf of, the former are largely excluded from the instrumental games of politics and power asymmetries of current democracy. They are thus far from the ideological imposition of the dominant discourse and may bring policy planners and stakeholders to deal with a different, and relatively autonomous, sphere of private and public, cultural and political, or even economic totality of attitudes and practices (Lears 1985: 571) which might substitute organic minority intellectuals to a newly formed leading form of actorness. In other words, operational policies targeting traditional minority intellectuals in the attempt to mobilise them may get rid of reinforcing subaltern conditions that organic minority intellectuals play with by keeping in check communities they represent. In other words, they are complicit to produce dependency through establishing internal hierarchies with those shelter-givers (e.g., NGOs, government bodies, civic movements, politics-oriented lobbyists) which too pursue their interests to maintain helplessness itself as such in order to secure their "humanitarian" protectorate. As briefly introduced, this is nothing more than what Laclau and Mouffe (1986) theorized with reference to a certain relation of subordination on a cultural level, which is patronising and purely colonising, and the relation of oppression on a political level, which sets apart certain subaltern voices and cultures inside those already dominated societal groups.

As the Sardinian philosopher pointed out, the presence of "organic" and "traditional" intellectuals is centrally paramount to understanding how subaltern voices are organically part of the hegemonic discourse which victimise them and others traditionally left out and set aside. This dichotomy, which remains problematic in the "Gramscian scholarship", sheds a new kind of light over the multi-layered and intersectional aspect of minority dynamics. As previously stated, the use of the paradigm of subalternity along with my proposal to use the distinction between the organic and traditional intellectuals with respectively "organic minority members" and "traditional minority members", does not only aim to indicate the discriminatory practices that flow from, and relate to, the social majority towards a given minority. Rather, it also evokes the hidden subaltern positions that a given minority is composed of from within. Understanding that the political agency of intellectuals does not represent a metaphysical actorness through their mobilisation, "organic minority members"—namely, representatives of government bodies, politicians, cultural gurus, religious institutions, NGO practitioners, and "experts" of all sorts— must be again differentiated from "traditional minority members"—namely, generally ordinary people—in order to better recognise those different and unheard claims and needs of the above-mentioned subaltern counter-publics. In doing so, once again, subalternity provides an instrument to tackle "too culturalist" and essentialist ascription of minority groups as homogenous and monolithic collective actors, giving thought to how different legal recognition and political possibilities are when in the hands of "organic minority members". This is extremely important to mobilise and active subaltern segments of society not exclusively along cultural lines, but only along political lines, which, in turn, do not nullify cultural and identity features.

However, once again, the entire dismissal of the role that organic intellectual minority members play in and out of the community they belong to, cannot be proposed or introduced. Yet, it has to be thought critically without falling into the trap of the political correctness. In fact, as Gramsci himself pointed out, everyone is an intellectual who holds a spontaneous philosophy which is proper to everyone. Therefore, their "organically" instrumental involvement is not what Gramsci referred to as "enjoyment of elements of hegemony". Rather, they selfishly establish interests-oriented interconnectedness with hegemony, creating some meaningful political and dialectical reciprocity in the form of publics and counter-publics, which, however, barely allows some modicum of accountability (Müller 2017: 46). In doing so, they simply ignore on purpose critical and anti-mainstream voices from within the same group they represent and speak on behalf of (e.g., subaltern counter-publics and hegemonic counter-publics). Instead, traditional minority intellectuals—also called "ordinary people" in the fields of sociology and anthropology—reveal more pragmatic and quotidian attitudes to deal with their subalternity by being less likely to become actors of potential turbulences or disloyalty. They tend in fact to respond more positively to their "situated otherness" in divisive contexts that set them apart. Since they live outside the power political structures they are governed by, they seem more likely to be immune to both the overwhelming dominant discourse of the State and to the one of organic minority intellectuals that they often mistrust by openly expressing diverse forms of quotidian political dissatisfaction.

In the second section of this conclusive section, looking beneath minority issues through subalternity, issues of "minority historicism" have been undertaken through Gramsci's concept of "organic crisis". The latter shows indeed the post-1989 minority positionality in Eastern Europe more as a culturally subaltern human condition than a political one. The lasting period of (organic) crisis that Gramsci referred to, definitely shows how the "post-Communist Pandoras Box" is still open and more problematic than it was in the early aftermaths of 1989, the "annus mirabilis" (Ahrens 2007: 536). In this post-Communist interregnum, as Gramsci would have eventually called it, it is no longer possible to affirm that Communism still exists. By default, it collapsed, and its post-1989 façade is more and more crumbling (Tamás 2009:35). However, a minority perspective of the post-1989 events shows how the Communist trajectory of power, which has not ceased to exist and influence the socio-cultural and political realm, has managed to persist throughout the collapse of the previous regime. This does not yet permit the old to die and the new to be born, leaving only space to an interregnum where morbid symptoms appear (Gramsci 1971: 276).

Although to a certain extent Gramsci's philosophy of praxis may seem to pursue similar goals than Charles Taylor's recognition (1993), the fact that any struggle is nowadays doomed to fail due to a wide range of "cultural identities" does not challenge little the liberal principle of the State whose neutrality cannot be questioned. On the contrary, moving beyond the normative horizon and approaching specific minority manners means to take into account the principle of full recognition and parity that equalizes all individuals and communities they potentially are members of. The latter, which emphasises cultural parity, deals historically with the issue of "recognisability" rather than "recognition".

In light of the vast articulation of subaltern claims and needs, in

Gramsci's terms, the term (re-)cognisability recalls the Middle Age Latin "cognosco", namely the capacity of knowing, or being aware of those people and cultures whom we have not heard of, of their history, of their literature, of their culture, and so forth. This "cognition" rejects a priori any kind of dismissal of certain knowledge, which has to be necessarily known in order to not be left out. Only through such (re)cognition, the capacity of unravelling historical contradictions (Gramsci 1953: 376) will shed light on problems of inclusion into the democratic arena, thereby brining out historically ranked hierarchies of ethnic, cultural, and racial forms of prejudices. In fact, in this action of recognisability lies the disruption of certain peoples' subalternity. Being aware of the presence and existence of different modes of living and existences allows all social groups to achieve social esteem and full dignity to live and flourish. It is here obvious that discourses, theories, and practices of and for coexistence have to be preceded by such recognisability of dignity in history prior to move forward and set up conditions of well-living.

Therefore, this new kind of "stepping back" is not aimed at assimilating backwardness into the energetic space of the social majority. Rather, it is aimed at stepping back for (re)cognising the foundations on which a society of equals has potentially yet to come. In order to do so, however, it is important to have recognisability of the hegemonic construction of post-Communist power blocs and how they came to power by subtly resurfacing from the past, at first setting the alien Other apart, and at second, securing dominant positions throughout changing social, political, economic, historical, and economic changes. A "minority perspective", indeed, sheds light clearly on how the most vulnerable societal groups (e.g., ethnic, gender, and LGBTQI+) that were exposed to benefit from a period of radical change after an epoch of invisibility, became instead those social categories that had only, in theory, the greatest window of opportunity, but, in practice, suffered the greatest losses during that historical epoch (Ilisei 2017: 57). Following Gramsci's historicism, issues of recognisability cannot be excluded from a serious reconciliation in history. Against the pitfall of "being-affected-by-the-past" (Paul Ricœur, mentioned by Kearny 1999: 82), subaltern micro-histories have been clearly set aside in the post-1989 "organic crisis" despite the fact they are extremely relevant even for the national history of a given country. Back to Gramsci's paradigm of "organic crisis", history cannot be only considered as a chronology-oriented procession of facts and events that peter out a specific historic-ideological epoch, such as Fukuyama's (1994). History, as Michel Foucault argued, reveals a separation between "effective history" and "traditional history". The collapse of the Eastern Bloc, which was an event of unique characteristics for minority groups across the region, highlighted an acute manifestation of history (Foucault 1977: 154), particularly of the principle of actuality whose force has played a negative role upon minority groups and cultures.

The dismissal of micro-histories from the official history is a direct result of the shift of power that began to occur in 1989; since then, the Daróczi-like question "Shouldn't We Have No History?" (2018: 20–35) represents the risk of lacking a fair transmission of historical (minority) experiences that are considered of no importance, and contingently considered as the dross of history (Gramsci 1971: 409). By leaving such narrative out in favour of a single perspective of history, disputes over political issues will continue repeatedly to empower those who dominantly control the discourse in the present at the expense of those who are ideologically controlled and politically governed by them. Therefore, it is here crucial the role that historians would play by showing their willingness to fully reconsider integrations of minority narratives into the "official (national) history" of a given country. This is, indeed, a centrally paramount mission to accomplish in the field of a multicultural educational system, among others. The opposite scenario may instead continue to dismiss certain segments of society from having the opportunities to publicly recollect their past experiences (e.g., selfidealisation) and the experiences they come from (Huntington and Harrison 2000: xx–xxi, quoted by Raud 2016: 390). It is not possible to get a grip on a potential society of cultural respect without recognisability of the multifaceted historical dimension (Kymlicka and Bashir 2008: 5), thereby neglecting the different roles that smaller and inconspicuous, albeit vivid and present, communities and cultures actively played in the past.

From this viewpoint, the issue of historical recognisability is a main cultural counteraction to organise against the potential pitfall of denying people in the past and disqualifying them in the present as a consequence. Following Gramsci's historicism, a counter-remedy for historical injustices and recognition of paper can shape, among other things, a social desire to advocate minority histories and their memories of a real society of parity differences. For example, as Gramsci wrote in defence of Armenians throughout one of the cruellest pages of the history of this population: "Armenians who find themselves scattered throughout Europe should make known their country, their history, their literature. [...] Armenians should make Armenia known, bring it alive for the uninformed, for those who do not know or pay heed" (Gramsci 1916).

Hence, once again, Chantal Mouffe's critique toward the "rationalist" liberal attitude of multiculturalism to impose counter-hegemonic weakly, gives credits to the denial discourse of historical and societal injustices which, however, are not meant to legitimise conflicts and disagreements as inherent phenomena of the democratic realm (Müller 2017: 53). Similarly, Slavoj Žižek, too, has argued that an anti-colonial type of defence of the multiplicity of identities in the past and present covers social antagonism and its force against economic inequality. The necessity of a "class struggle", which multiculturalism would seem to officially promote under the mantra "sex-class-race", never impinges actually on the concrete inequalities of our society (2018: 189,220). Both can be cheaply bought from a Gramscian perspective.

However, introducing "subalternity" is meant to keep away any conspicuous and vernacular political project that has potentially been widespread among the scholarly circles of Marxology, post-colonial studies, Critical Theory, and so forth. In order to better clarify this fundamental result of this current study, minority members and practitioners must work together on strategies aiming at setting up "a dialogue". The latter, in turn, has to be extremely confrontational between "coercion", which is the force that imposes cultural hegemony throughout society, and "consent", that is, the construction of a (political) persuasion aimed at leading the emergence of a counter-hegemonic bloc of critical voices, touchy instances, alternative practices, and confrontational attitudes towards autonomous institutions for a society to come. Following Gramsci, the social actorness of the civil society is not only fundamental for leaving space to a de-colonialised place of existence, but also for representing an emancipatory non-physical space of counteraction and confrontation. Aware of Gramsci's philosophical ambiguity over the so-called "statolatry", subalternity democratically and fairly exacerbates the democratic confrontation between the State and the civil society's actors that contemporary "hegemons" have successfully avoided by instrumentally keeping the dominated groups in check and at their disposal. To partially conclude this point, both consent and "coercion" mean hegemony, namely, *leading leadership* for turning all particularities into the universal throughout a process of becoming "macro".

As also Kymlicka honestly pointed out, multiculturalism is only possible to establish within a well-rooted form of constitutionalism in tandem with a long-term democratic tradition of the society where it would be proposed and simply applied. Therefore, considering that the post-Communist Europe region possesses neither a long-term tradition of democratic experience nor yet a full-fledged democracy, constitutional reform(s) might pave the way to a constructively open-ended contestation of the current constitutional structures that post-Communist CEE's *ethnocist* Nations are based on[3].

Among others, the Republic of Armenia is a positive example to mention in in this case. Despite the fact that the country, formerly the Soviet Socialist Republic of Armenia, has been historically a mono-ethnic country, since 2005 the political system began vigorously campaigning to guarantee enough judicial recognition to non-Armenian inhabitants belonging to ethnic minorities. Armenia's ethnic minority groups have never been in the position to challenge the central supremacy, yet their participation in the constitutional reforms and amendments has played a positive role. Although issues with other subaltern groups (e.g., feminism discourse, LGBTQI+ community, peacemakers against the frozen conflicts and alike) remain a concern in the country, these constitutional reforms have given to the country an opportunity for its democratic institutions, still-in-transition, to promote political legitimacy and transparency among societal groups, more respect of fundamental rights, and integrative paths for public policies. Although there might be cultural hesitation to recognise subaltern diversities due to historical and moral tradition, constitutional reforms might rebalance the entire arena of democracy (e.g., publics/counter-publics/subaltern counter-publics), facilitating the post-Communist "organic crisis" to dock into the port of full-fledged democracy and opening the door to a serious confrontational debate and struggle for fully equal parity principles among societal groups and individuals who do or do not want to be part of it—no matter if majorities or minorities, subalterns or hegemons.

In fact, citizens have to think of themselves as equally recognised actors able to respond to unsuspected appeals of being represented, and all of a sudden see themselves as a collective actor, as individuals capable of acting in concert, as Hannah Arendt's famous expression continues proudly to echo nowadays.

---

[3] *Ibidem*, Gáspár Miklós Tamás, cit., Public Lecture "A New Fascism".

Bibliography

Abeysekara, A. (2011). The Un-Translatability of Religion, the UnTranslatability of Life: Thinking Talal Asad's Thought Unthought. In "Method and Theory in the Study of Religion", Vol. 23, Pp: 257-282.

Ahrens, G. (2007) Diplomacy on the Edge: Containment of Ethnic and the Minorities Working Group of the Conference on Yugoslavia, Washington/D.C.: MD.

Ali, S. (2004). Mixed-Race, Post-Race: Gender, New Ethnicities and Cultural Practices. London: Berg.

Althusser, L. (1976). Essays in Self-Criticism, London: New Left Books.

Antonio Gramsci 1891-1937 (1994) The Formation of Intellectuals, in Kearney, R., and Rainwater, M. (Ed.) The Continental Philosophy Reader, London: Routledge, Pp. 181-197.

Ayunts, A., Zalyan, M., and Zakaryan, T. (2016) Nagorny-Karabarakh Conflict: Prospects for Conflict Transformation, The Journal of Nationalism and Ethnicity, London: Routledge.

Badiou, A., Bourdieu, P., Butler, J., Didi-Huberman, G., Khiari, S., Rancière, J. (2016) What is A People? New York: Columbia University Press.

Baev, J. (2015). De-Stalinisation and Political Rehabilitation in Bulgaria. In McDermott, K., Stibbe, M., (Ed.) De-Stalinising Eastern Europe. The Rehabilitation of Stalin's Victims after 1953, Hampshire: Palgrave Macmillan, Pp. 150-169.

Baggini, J. (2018). How the World Thinks. A Global History of Philosophy, London: Granta.

Bakalian, A. (1993). Armenian-Americans. From Being to Feeling Armenian, New Brunswick - New Jork: Transaction.

Barth, F. (1969) Introduction. In Barth, F. (Ed.) Ethnic Groups and Boundaries: The Social Organization of Culture Difference, Boston: Little Brons.

Bayadyan, H., (2012) Becoming Post-Soviet, Hatje Cantz, Series: Documenta (13) P. 100.

Bebgy, E., Burgees, P. (2009) Human Security and Liberal Peace. In: Journal of Political and Moral Philosophy, Volume I, Number I, Pp. 91-104.

Benhabib, S. (2002) The Claims of Culture Equality and Diversity in the Global Era, Princeton: Princeton University Press.

Blackbrun, R. (2014) On Stuart Hall (1932-2014). In: New Left Review, 86, Mar/Apr, London, Pp. 75-95.

Billig, M. (1995) Banal Nationalism. London: Sage.

Birnbaum, A. (2016) The Obscure Object of Transdisciplinarity. Adorno on the Essay Form. In: Radical Philosophy (198) Pp. 15-24.

Bogomilova, N. (2015) Religion in a Secular Context: Balkan Projections. Sofia: Paradigma.

Braueunlein, J. P. (2014) Postcolonial Theory. In: Jesudas, A. (Ed.) Religion and Southeast Asia: An Encyclopaedia of Faiths and Cultures. Santa Barbara: ABC Clio, Pp. 1-8.

Braude, B., and Lewis, B. (1982) Christians and Jews in the Ottoman Empire: The Functioning of a Plural Society. New York: Lynne Rienner Publishers.

Butler, J., Laclau E., Žižek, S. (2000) Contingency, Hegemony, Universality.

Contemporary Dialogue on the Left. London: Verso.
Castellino, J. (2018) Identity and Human Rights in a "Populist" Era: Urging Caution and Pragmatism in Minority Rights Protection. In: Anna-Mária Bíró (Ed.) Populism, Memory, and Minority Rights. Central and Eastern European Issues in Global Perspective, Leiden: Brill, Pp. 342-356
Chappell, S. G. (2018) Being Transgender and Transgender Being. In: Pietrzak, P. (Ed.) In Statu Nascendi – Journal of Political Philosophy and International Relations (1,1) Pp. 19-30.
Chérif, M. (2008) Islam and the West: A Conversation with Jacques Derrida, Chicago: University of Chicago Press.
Cheskin, A. (2016) Russian Speakers in Post-Soviet Latvia. Discursive Identity Strategy. Edinburgh: Edinburgh University Press.
Chomsky, N. (1999) The New Military Humanism. Lessons from Kosovo. London: Pluto Press.
Ciovolella, R. (2013) Looking for Gramsci in Local Resistances – Reflections from the Margins. Paper presented at the panel Capitalism and Global Anthropology: Marxism Resurgent at the 17th Conference of the International Union of Anthropological and Ethnological Studies, 5th-10th, Manchester, UK.
Cohen, P. (2018) Archive That, Comrade! Left legacies and the Counter Culture of Remembrance, Oakland: PM Press.
Cornell, Stephen, Hartmann, Douglas. Ethnicity and Race. Making Identities in a Changing World, London: Pine Forge Press, 1998.
Craib, I. (1998) Experiencing Identity, London: Sage.
Daróczi, Á. (2018) Shouldn't We Have No History? In: Anna-Mária Bíró (Ed.) Populism, Memory, and Minority Rights. Central and Eastern European Issues in Global Perspective, Leiden: Brill, Pp. 20-35.
Dawson, J. (2016) Cultures of Democracy in Serbia and Bulgaria. How ideas Shape Publics, London: Routledge.
Deleuze, G., Guattari, F. (1986) Kafka. Toward a Minor Literature, Minneapolis and London: University of Minnesota Press.
Elster, J. (1994) Constitutional Politics and Economic Transformation in PostCommunist. A Comparative Study of Bulgaria, Czechoslovakia and Hungary, UK: Edward Elgar Publishing.
Emilova, S. (2017) Islamophia in Bulgaria. In: Bayrakly, E., Hafez, F. (Ed.) European Islamophobia Report 2017, Istanbul: SETA | Foundation for Political, Economic and Social Research, Pp. 127-142.
Erdaği, B. (2014) Karl Heinrich Marx and Political Philosophy, in: Sophia Philosophical Review (8) No.1, Pp. 34-69.
Fanon, F. (2011) The Wretched of the Earth, London: Penguin Book.
Finkelde, D. (2013) Post-Structuralism. In: New Catholic Encyclopaedia Supplement - Section "Ethics and Philosophy", Vol. 3, Pp. 12451248.
Foejtö, F. (1974) A History of the People's Democracies. Eastern Europe Since Stalin. Middlesex: Penguin Books.
Foucault, M. (1971) Nietzsche, Genealogy and History, Oxford: Backwell
Foucault, M. (1980) Power/Knowledge. Selected Interview and Other Writing 1972-7. In: King, A. (2005) Spaces of Global Cultures. Architecture,

Urbanism, Identity, UK: Routledge.

Fraser, N. (1992) Rethinking the Public Sphere: A Contribution to the Critique of Actually Existing Democracy. In: Calhoun, C. (Ed.) Habermas and the Public Sphere, Massachusetts: MIT Press.

Fukuyama, F. (1992) The End of History and the Last Man. New York: The Free Press.

Fukuyama, F. (2011) The Origins of Political Order. From Prehuman Times to the French Revolution, New York: Straus & Giroux.

Fukuyama, F. (2018) Identity. Contemporary Identity Politics and the Struggle for Recognition. London: Profile Books.

Gayatri, C. S. (1992) 'Interview with Gayatri Chakravorty Spivak: New Nation Writers Conference in South Africa. Interview Conducted by L. De Kock', *Ariel: A Review of International English Literature* 23(3).

Glavanakova, A. (2016) Trans-Cultural Imaginings. Translating the Other, Translating the Self in Narratives about Migration and Terrorism. Sofia: Critique and Humanism Publishing House.

Goina, C. (2015) Rehabilitation in Romania: The Case of Lucrețiu Pătrășcanu. In: McDermott, K., Stibbe, M. (Eds.) De-Stalinising Eastern Europe. The Rehabilitation of Stalin's Victims after 1953, Hampshire: Palgrave Macmillan, Pp. 132-149.

Gramsci, A. (1971) Selection from Prison Notebooks. In: Hoare, Q., Smith, G. N. (Eds. and transl.) London: Lawrence and Wishart. Independent Radical Publishing.

Gramsci, A. (1916) Armenia 1915. Article published in "L'urlo del Popolo" dated March 11, 1916, Turin, Italy.

Green, M. (2011) 'Rethinking the Subaltern and the Question of Censorship in Gramsci's Prison Notebooks'. In: *Postcolonial Studies*, Vol. 14, No. 4, Pp. 387-404.

Goldenberg, S. (1994) Pride of Small Nations. The Caucasus and Post-Soviet Disorder, London: Zed Books Ltd.

Gržinić, M. (2019) Theorizing Decoloniality in Southeast Europe: Vocabularies, Politics, Perspectives. In: Decolonial Theory and Practice in Southeast Europe, Special Issue (3) Pp. 7-29.

Gržinić, M. (2000) Fiction Reconstructed: Eastern Europe, Post-socialism and the Retro-Avant-Garde, Vienna: Springerin.

Hadjian, A. (2018) Secret Nation: The Hidden Armenians of Turkey, London: IB Taurus.

Hall, S. (1987) Gramsci and Us. Paper published in Marxism Today.

Harris, S., Nawaz, M. (2015) Islam and the Future of Tolerance. A Dialogue. Massachusetts: Harvard University Press.

Heidegger, M. (1969) Identity and Difference (transl. by Stambaugh Joan) Chicago: The University of Chicago Press.

Henry, M. G. (2003) 'Where Are You Really From?' Representation, Identity and Power in the Fieldwork Experience of a South Asian Diasporic. In: Qualitative Research, Vol. 3(2), London: SAGE Publications, Pp. 229242.

Hobsbawm, E. (1983) Introduction in Hobsbawm. In: Ranger, T. (Ed.) The Interpretation of Tradition, Cambridge: Cambridge University Press.

Hovhannisyan, S., Mkrtchyan, N., Merjian, A. (2016) Gramsci's Circle of Humanity and Armenia, Yerevan: Armenian Association of World History.

Hys, D. (2004) A Critical Assessment of Will Kymlicka's Theory of Minority Rights: Dilemmas of Liberal Multiculturalism. Master's Degree thesis published in the website of Toronto University, Fall 2014, http://www.collectionscanada.gc.ca/obj/thesescanada/vol2/002/MR17790.PDF

Ilisei, I. (2017) Romania: A Missed Opportunity for Minorities. In: Slaukova, L. (Ed.) Mapping Transition in Eastern Europe: Experiences of Change after the End of Communism, Berlin: German-Russian Exchange (DRA e.V.) Pp. 57-67.

Isaacs, H. (1975) Idols of the Tribe: Group Identity and Political Chance. Cambridge, MA: Harvard University Press.

Laitin, D. (1998) Identity in Formation. The Russian Speaking Populations in the Near Abroad, London: Cornell University Press, Pp. 10-16.

Lears, T. J. (1985) The Concept of Cultural Hegemony: Problems and Possibilities. In: The American Historical Review, Oxford University Press, Vol. 90, No. 3, Pp. 567-593.

Lyotard, J. (1983) The Post-Modern Condition: A Report on Knowledge. In: Bennington, G., Massumi, B., (transl by.) Theory and History of Literature (10) Minneapolis: University of Minnesota Press.

Lenin, V. (1972) The Right of Nations to Self-Determination. In: Isaacs, B., Fineberg, J. (transl. by) Collected Works (20) Moscow: Progress Publishers, Pp. 393-454.

Jenkins, P. (2007) God's Continent. Christianity, Islam and Europe's Religious Crisis, Oxford: Oxford University Press.

Jenkins, R. (1996) Social identity, London: Routledge.

Thede, K. (2002) The Ethnicity of Aromanians After the 1990: The Identity of a Minority that Behaves Like a Majority. In: Ethonologia Balkanica (6) Sofia: Prof. Marin Drinov Academic Publishing House, Pp. 145-169.

Karkov, N., Valiavicharska, Z. (2018) Rethinking East-European Socialism: Notes Toward an Anti-Capitalist Decolonial Methodology Interventions. In: Decolonial Theory and Practice in Southeast Europe, Special Issue (03) Pp. 785-813.

Asim, K., Anjum, R. Y. (2016) Multiculturalism and Post-Structural Theory: Appraisal and Implications. In: Gomal University Journal of Research (32, 1) Pp. 33-43.

Kearney, R. (1999) Poetics of Modernity. Toward a Hermeneutic Imagination, New York: Humanity Books, Pp. 80-92.

Kirvelyté, L. (2015) The Conflict of Nagorno-Karabakh: Is There A Way to "Unfreeze" The Resolution Process? In: The Margins of the NagornoKarabakh Conflict: In Search of Solution, Centre for Geopolitical Studies (Ed.), Vilnius.

Kołodziejczyk, D. (2010) Post-Colonial Transfer to Central-and-Eastern Europe, in: "Teksty Drugie" (5) Pp. 124-142.

König, T. (2001) The Hegemony of Multiculturalism. A Comment on Will Kymlicka's Theory of Nationalism. In: Politička Misao, Vol. XXXVIII, N.5,

Pp. 48-61.

Kovačević, N. (1998) Narrating Post/Communism: Colonial Discourse and Europe's Borderline Civilization, Abington – New York: Routledge, Pp. 11-20.

Kramnick, J. (2017) The Interdisciplinary Fallacy. In: Representations (140) Pp. 67-83.

Krasniqi, G. (2010) The International Community's Modus Operandi in Postwar Bosnia and Herzegovian and Kosovo: A Critical Assessment. In Südosteuropa (58) Jahrgang: Heft, Pp. 520 -541.

Kul-Want, C. (2013) Introducing Continental Philosophy. A Graphic Guide, London: Omnibus Business Centre, Pp. 123-124.

Kundera, M. (1984) The Tragedy of Central Europe. In: White, Edmund (transl. by) New York Review of Books, Volume 31, Number 7, Pp. 1-14.

Kushnir, O. (2018) Ukraine and Russian Neo-Imperialism. The Divergent Break. Lanham: Lexington Books.

Kušić, K., Lottholz, P., Manolova, P. (2019) From Dialogue to Practice: Pathways towards Decoloniality in Southeast Europe. In: Decolonial Theory and Practice in Southeast Europe, Special Issue, 03, Pp. 7-29.

Kymlicka, W., Bashir, B. (2010) The Politics of Reconciliation in Multicultural Societies, Oxford: Oxford University Press.

Kymlicka, W., Opalski, M. (2000) Can Liberal Pluralism be Exported? Western Political Theory and Ethnic Relations in Eastern Europe. Oxford: Oxford University Press.

Kymlicka, W., Marín, R. (1999) Liberalism and Minority Rights. In: Ratio Juris Journal, 12, no. 2, Pp. 133-52.

Kymlicka, W. (1995) Multicultural Citizenship. A Liberal Theory of Minority Rights. Oxford: Clarendon Press.

Kymlicka, W. (1992) Two Models of Pluralism and Tolerance. In: Analyse & Kritik (13) Pp. 32-56.

Laclau, E., Mouffe, C. (1985) Hegemony and Socialist Strategy: Towards a Radical Democratic Politics, London: Verso.

Laclau, E. (1994) The Making of Political Identities, London and New York: Verso.

Leview-Sawyer, C. (2015) Bulgaria: Politics and Protests in the 21th Century. Sofia: Riva.

Marchart, O. (2018) Thinking Antagonism. Political Ontology after Laclau. Edinburgh: Edinburgh University Press.

Mahmuti, B. (2015) Blood Libel. Anti-Americanism and Genocide in the Kosovo War, Pristina: Çabej.

Makariev, P. (2017) The Public Legitimacy of Minority Claims: A Central/Eastern European perspective, UK: Routledge.

Marinov, M. (2017) Religious Communities in Bulgaria, Blagoevgrad: SouthWest Bulgaria University Publishing House.

Matuštík, J. M. (1993) Post-National Identity. Critical Theory and Existential Philosophy in Habermas, Kierkegaard, and Havel, London: The Guilford Press.

McDermott, K., Pinerová, K. (2015) The Rehabilitation Process in

Czechoslovakia: Party and Popular Responses. In: McDermott, K., Stibbe, M. (Eds.) De-Stalinising Eastern Europe. The Rehabilitation of Stalin's Victims after 1953, Hampshire: Palgrave Macmillan, Pp. 109-131.

Merdjanova, I. (2006) Uneasy Tolerance: Interreligious Relations after the Fall of Communism. In: Religion in Eastern Europe – Christian Associated for Relations with Eastern Europe, Vol. XXVI, No. 1, Pp. 1-11.

Meyer, J. (2002) De La Violence à la Religion: Aller-Retour. In: Social Compass, No.49(2), Pp. 203-212.

Mouffe, C. (2000) Politics and Passions: The Stakes of Democracy. In: Ethical Perspectives, 7 (2-3), Pp. 148-150.

Müller, J. (2017) What is Populism?, London: Penguin Books.

Multiculturalism. Stanford Encyclopedia of Philosophy, (Last Modified August 12) 2016.
https://stanford.library.sydney.edu.au/archives/win2015/entries/multiculturalism/

Murray. Douglas (2018) The Strange Death of Europe. Immigration, Identity, Islam. London: Bloomsbury Continuum.

Nail, T. (2015) The figure of the Migrant, Boulder: Colorado University Press.

Nałęcz, D. (2018) The Evolution and Implementation of the Intermarium Strategy in Poland: A Historical Perspective. in: Kushnir, O. (Ed.) The Intermarium as the Polish-Ukrainian Linchpin of Baltic-Black Sea Cooperation, Cambridge: Cambridge Scholars Publishing, Pp. 1-21.

Naumović, S. (2002) The Ethnology of Transformation as Transformed Ethnology: The Serbian Case. In: Ethnologia Balkanica, Vol. 6, Sofia: Prof. Marin Drinov Academic Publishing House, Pp. 7-36.

Norton. B. (2000) Identity and Language Learning, Harlow England: Pearson Education, Ltd., Pp. 125-127.

Pentassuglia, G. (2018) Group Identities and Human Rights: How Do We Square the Circle in International Law?. In: Anna-Mária Bíró (Ed.) Populism, Memory, and Minority Rights. Central and Eastern European Issues in Global Perspective, Leiden: Brill, Pp. 283-312.

Quijano, A. (2000) Coloniality of Power, Eurocentrism, and Latin America, Nepantla: Views from South 1(3), Pp. 533-580.

Rácz, K. (2017) The Return of the Ethnic? Multiculturalism from an Ethnic Minority Perspective. In: "Filozofija i Društvo", XXVIII (2), Pp. 377-394.

Rancière, J. (1995) On the Shores of Politics. London: Verso Books.

Randazzo, E. (2015) Changing Narrative? Shifting Discursive Conceptualisations of Post-Conflict Peace-Building. PhD dissertation published in the website of the University of Westminster (UK) https://westminsterresearch.westminster.ac.uk/item/973xz/changing-narratives-shifting-discursive-conceptualisations-of-post-conflict-peace-building

Raud, R. (2016) Zygmunt Bauman's Critique of Multiculturalism: A Polemical Reading. In: Revue Internationale de Philosophie, (3) Pp. 381-397.

Rexhepi, P. (2018) Unmapping Islam in Eastern Europe: Periodization and Muslim Subjectivities in the Balkans. In: Kacandes, I., Komska, Y., (Eds.) Eastern Europe Unmapped: Beyond Borders and Peripheries, New York:

Berghahn, Pp. 53-78.

Robertson, G. (2006) Crimes against Humanity. The Struggle for Global Justice, New York: The New Press.

Salecl, R. (1994) The Spoils of Freedom. Psychoanalysis and Feminism After the Fall of Socialism, London: Routledge, Pp. 11-19.

Saini, A. (2019) Superior. The Return of Race Science, London: 4th Estate.

Schwandener-Sievers, S. (2019) Introduction. In: Armakolas, I., Demjaha, A., Elbasani, A., Schwandener-Sievers, S. (Eds.) Local and International Determinants of Kosovo's Statehood, Pristina: Kosovo Foundation for Open Society (KFOS), Pristina, Pp. 21-22, https://kfos.org/local-and-international-determinants-of-kosovos-statehood/

Selden, R (1998) The Theory of Criticism. From Plato to the Present, London: Longman.

Shenk, G. (2006) What Went Right: Two Best Case of Islam in Europe. In: Religion in Eastern Europe – Christian Associated for Relations with Eastern Europe, Vol. XXVI, No. 4, Pp. 7-20.

Smith, B. (2016) Poststructuralist Theory of Identity: Its Framework and Implications for Language Learning. In: "目白大学 人文学研究, 第",12号, Pp.253-263.

Soldado, M. F. (2019) The Angel of Nostalgia Trapped Between East and West. In: Doğan, E. (Ed.) Reiventing Eastern Europe: Imaginaries, Identities and Transformations, London: Transnational Press London, Pp. 9-23.

Spickard D. (2010) Religion, Human Rights and Global Culture. A Dozen Years Later. In: Philosophical Alternative, No.5, Pp. 120-134.

Spivak, G. C. (1999) A Critique of Postcolonial Reason. Toward a History of the Vanishing Present, Harvard: Harvard University Press.

Spivak, G. C. (1988) Can the Subaltern Speak?. In: Nelson, C., Grossberge, L. (Eds.) Marxism and the Interpretation of Culture, Urbana: University of Illinois.

Strinati, D. (1995) An Introduction to Theories of Popular Culture, London: Routledge.

Terian, A. (2012) Is there an East-Central European Post-Colonialism? Towards a Unified Theory of (Inter)Literacy Dependency. In: World Literature Studies, (3, 4) Pp. 21-36.

Tamás, G. M. (2009) Hungary: When We Were Wrong. In: Harman, C. (Ed.) International Socialism (123) London: Information Press, Pp. 27-40;

Tillich, P. (2000) Systematic Theology. In: Universitetskaya Kniga (2) Moscow, P. 23.

Tlostanova, M. (2019) Towards a Decolonization of Thinking and Knowledge: a Few Reflections from the World of Imperial Difference. In: Decolonial Theory and Practice in Southeast Europe, Special Issue, 03, P.186.

Tlostanova, M. (2004) Post-Soviet Literature and the Aestesthic of Transculturalism, "Two Decades After the Wall's Fall. End of Communism Cheered but Now More Reservations", The Pew Global Project Attitudes, Washington DC.

Vavřík, M. (2010) The Three Theses of Jürgen Habermas. In: Sophia Philosophical Review, Volume IV, No.1, Pp. 101-113.

Velikonja, M. (2003) Religion in Eastern Europe, College Station Texas – University Press.

Vilić, N. (2000) State _ Irwin, Skopje: 3590 Network of Local and Subaltern Hermeneutics.

Viola, F. (2002) The Links of Community According to Liberalism and Communitarianism. In: Banús, E., Llan, A., (Eds.) Present and Future of Liberalism, Barañáin: Eunsa, Pp.521-533.

Warner, M. (2002) Publics and Counterpublics, Public Culture. In: Project MUSE, Vol. 14 No. 1, Pp. 49-90.

Waldron, J. (2000a) Cultural Identity and Civic Responsibility. In: Kymlicka, W., Norman, N. (Eds.) Citizenship in Diverse Societies, New York: Oxford University Press.

Waligore, T. (2009) Cosmopolitan Rights, Indigenous People, and the Risks of Cultural Interaction. In: Journal of Political and Moral Philosophy, Volume I, Number I, Pp. 27-56.

Winchester, S. (1999) The Fracture Zone. A Return to the Balkans, London: Viking Publishing.

Wunsh, N. (2018) EU Enlargement and Civil Society in the Western Balkans. From Mobilisation to Empowerment, Zurich: Palgrave Macmillan.

Zhamakochyan, A. Armenia in the trap of "national unity". Article published in TransConflict (February 20, 2017) http://www.transconflict.com/2017/02/armenia-inthe-trap-of-national-unity-102/).

Žižek, S. (2018) The Courage of Hopelessness. Chronicles of a Year of Acting Dangerously, London: Penguin Books.

Žižek, S. (1993) Es Gibt Keinen Staat in Europee. In: Vilić, N. (Ed.) State_Irwin, Skopje: 3590 Network of Local and Subaltern Hermeneutics, Pp. 135-158.

www.ingramcontent.com/pod-product-compliance
Lightning Source LLC
Chambersburg PA
CBHW051542230426
43669CB00015B/2690